ALWAYS WHOLE

An LDS Perspective on Being While Becoming

Paul Peterson, MA, LPC, LMFT

This work is solely for personal growth and education. It should not be treated as a substitute for professional assistance, therapeutic activities such as psychotherapy or counseling, or medical advice. In the event of physical or mental distress, please consult with appropriate health professionals. The application of protocols and information in this book is the choice of each reader, who assumes full responsibility for his or her understanding, interpretations, and results. The author and publisher assume no responsibility for the actions or choices of any reader.

Audiobook listeners: Please see the accompanying PDF for helpful images, tables, and footnotes.

The clinical examples in this book are composites of client themes, not actual session transcriptions in order to preserve client confidentiality and privacy.

Thich Nhat Hanh, "Please Call Me by My True Names" from *Call Me By My True Names: The Collected Poems of Thich Nhat Hanh*. Copyright © 1999 by Unified Buddhist Church. Reprinted with the permission of The Permissions Company, LLC on behalf of Parallax Press, Berkeley, California, parallax.org.

Cover design by Heidi Robertson
Book design and images by Paul Peterson
ISBN 979-8-9918694-0-9

To Wynn & Jocelyn (the ones who made me),
Anna (the one who holds me),
and Riv, Ev, & Bo (the ones who depend on me).

With deep gratitude

Contents

Part I: Becoming and Being

Part II: The Work

Part III: The Latter-day Saint Path

A PERSONAL NOTE

It's important for me to note where my expertise lies, and where it doesn't. I work as a Licensed Professional Counselor as well as a Licensed Marriage and Family Therapist in Bentonville, Arkansas. I run my own private practice and have given training to other therapists in hypnotherapy and private practice business coaching. Although I'll mention some themes around emotions, beliefs, trauma, and psychological transformation in this book, none of it is intended to be therapy or to replace working with a licensed professional. I have changed the personal details of any clients mentioned.

In addition to pursuing a career in psychotherapy, I also hope to live an examined, intentional life. This includes meditation training, contemplative Christianity, and other spiritual and transpersonal practices. I haven't been certified officially in any of these spiritual or meditative traditions. As such, I will point you to people who have more depth than I do in these areas if you'd like to learn more.

My church heritage includes a first-generation mother whose family joined the Church when she was ten, as well as a father who has deep lines in Latter-day Saint history. I grew up in a tiny ward in Granville, Ohio and then in a bigger ward in Bentonville, Arkansas beginning halfway through my high school years. I studied at BYU, served a mission in Finland, married in the temple, and have held a variety of callings.

I've had times of really cherishing the Church and times of disdaining or grieving it.

I am sharing all of this from a place of active exploration. I'm a student of many of these teachings, not a sanctioned teacher. These are my current experiences, peer to peer, that I share as a celebration of what's possible for interested students, even as they're in the early phases of a path like this one. The world is wide open.

I will do my best not to pretend I know more than I do. What I "know" seems to change all the time, anyway. Whatever your experience in reading this content, please know that my highest intentions are simply to share what goodness I've received from those much further on the path. My hope is to help you see something in the world around you as a little brighter, a bit more generous, and a touch more sacred, to enrich the life you're experiencing now.

INTRODUCTION

How would you answer this question: Is it better to be exactly who you are right now, or to become someone different?

To be honest, the way the question is framed is quite unsatisfying. On one hand, if I accept exactly who I am right now, aren't I leaving a lot of future potential unmet? Isn't the whole point of the gospel to strive, to become better, more holy, more like God? And sometimes I just don't like everything about myself—I want to be different. When I do change, transform, or grow, I feel deep satisfaction and accomplishment in the moment.

On the other hand, right now, I can really only be exactly who and what I am. Whether I like it or not doesn't change what's in this moment. What's more, there seem to be messy consequences for a stance of self-rejection, self-loathing, or self-distancing. I feel very unsettled when I constantly judge myself. Other times, though, I genuinely love being me, exactly as I am, here and now. Those moments are treasures. "Be still, and know that I am God."[1] Resting in my innate being seems essential.

---

1 D&C 101:16

NO WINNER

Being and becoming are like two modes in a human's life. They are conditions from which our hearts and minds can operate. But, one doesn't have to win over the other. In my experience, the answer to our introductory question is not a simple choice between two options. If only one side rules the roost, the imbalance knocks something meaningful out of the nest of our soul. Sometimes we have a greater need to be than to become, and other times we need the opposite. There are even times when they work together or can feel like the same thing.[2]

Early in childhood, it seemed like I could simply rest on the side of being who I was and not care a bit—playing, running, eating, laughing, crying, just going through life as one big moment of being, being, being. I was a really good human being for those early years. It was a present, engaged, in-the-moment regenerative trust[3] of just living to live, without having an internal narration of my life or worrying about what came next.

Then somewhere along the way, becoming increased in importance. I started to feel like I had to *do* certain things at certain times, in certain ways—as if there was a path I was supposed to walk. Some of this was probably inspired by my parents, who are genuinely amazing, and some from culture, society, church, evolutionary impulses, etc. My next phase of life, with a primary focus on becoming, lasted decades. It had high highs and low lows, and overall I'm happy I had that focus.

Eventually, though, I burned out of trying to continually become something all the time. It was so hard to feel really fulfilled, grounded, and satisfied when there was always something else to become, do, or achieve. I think what was happening was that I became unbalanced. It's exhausting to always need to be more, more, more! I grew up in the Church of Jesus Christ of

---

2 John Kesler, *Integral Polarity Practice in Service of Leadership for Flourishing.*

3 Rick Jarow, *Creating the Work You Love: Courage, Commitment, and Career.*

Latter-day Saints, where we often sing popular hymns about how much more we can become. In fact, in one hymn, we mention this becoming mode twenty-four times in under three minutes. Here's a sample:[4]

> More purity give me,
> More strength to o'ercome,
> More freedom from earth-stains,
> More longing for home.
> More fit for the kingdom,
> More used would I be,
> More blessed and holy—
> More, Savior, like thee.

Hymns like these, from a place of striving and not-enoughness, are debilitating! (However, if we sing this from a place of wholeness, it's an entirely different story, as we'll soon find out...) If I had to map my life energy from my mid-teens to late twenties, it would look something like this:

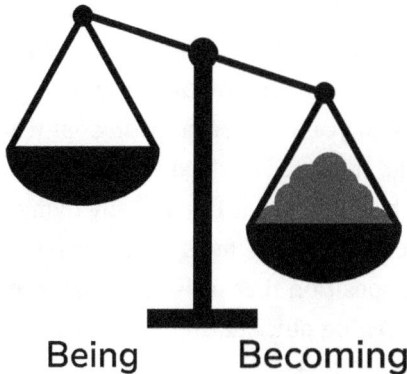

Being   Becoming

Toward the end of my twenties, I think I became imbalanced and entered burnout mode. However, I did accomplish what was on my becoming checklist: I got the education, the job, the house, a wife I cherish, and some beautiful kids. It was joyous, but also

---

4 Hymn 131

very hectic sometimes. Eventually, things began settling down, without many highs or lows, and I noticed feeling bland most of the time. One day as I was biking to work, I realized that all my energy for many years had been consumed with pining and working toward the future. But now, that future was here. I had done what I'd set out to do. I'd dropped the One Ring into Mount Doom. Now what? I didn't have a new way of being after I had become. I didn't know how to *enjoy* what I had become because I wasn't used to being present with what was, stopping to say: "This is enough."[5]

I know I'm not alone in having felt this way. I've heard common sentiments in many LDS circles: *I feel like there's always more to do... My bishop says I'm worthy, but I know there's really more I can do... Even when I'm alone in my house, I feel like someone is going to judge me if I take a minute just to sit down...* Certainly, these experiences aren't unique to church members, nor are they all due to church practices, teachings, or culture. But, sometimes it feels like there's an extra edge to Latter-day Saint fervor (or franticness) in becoming like God. After all, eternity is on the line! The pressure to drive without ceasing has consumed many LDS people I know, both personal friends and clients of mine, seeming to rob them of the capacity to be still and enjoy life now.

The past several years I've been testing out what leaning back into being can do. It's made all the difference for me. I feel like life just got a little brighter—that I'm actually living life in a meaningful way again. Becoming feels different too, and I approach it with a new disposition that feels sustainable and healthy. I'm recalibrating, evening out, and finding goodness anew.

---

5 Brandon Sanderson, *Oathbringer.*

HOLDING BOTH

It seems that I naturally took turns inhabiting each side of the scale—being and becoming—to really taste each deeply. Now, there seems to be a perspective I can take that holds the pair of them in equal regard. I've found that bringing both into life allows me to feel whole, satisfied, and complete each and every day, while also still allowing me to improve and walk a gospel path.

Since I was deficient in the being experience, pursuing it anew was a total revelation for me. I found a deep well from which I can source my intentions and actions. From an LDS perspective, it's like the Atonement or the infinite love of God, a source of terrific abundance, virtue, peace, and all other fruits of the Spirit. It can also take on qualities of the rest of the Lord, at least as I understand it.

Ironically, it seems like my focus on becoming eventually ran its course and prevented me from tapping into those deeper sacred waters. When that happened, life dried up for me. I felt irritated and perpetually unsettled or distracted—despite my best efforts to become what I was supposed to—and life just seemed off in some way. As I've allowed being to be a bigger part of my everyday life, it has also revitalized my capacity to transform and become, again, without the burnout.

When we can hold both in their fullness, we are unified with Divinity. We become extremely available to ourselves, others, and the moment. When I find a way to hold and relate to both being and becoming, I feel my mortal stuckness dissolving and a burst of divine virtue flows through me without effort and without end.

SAINTS IN BALANCE

Have you met any Saints who seem to live from this balance point? They are fully at peace with who they are, while being open to becoming something new every day. I've met several, and it's life-changing. They feel fully alive, completely available to the moment, and very divine. They are also very normal and usually non-descript, so if I'm not listening, I might not really hear them.

It's been my experience that the Church does a great job in many areas to help us cultivate a sacred heart, a keen mind, and willing hands. There are also numerous issues in the Church— incomplete ways we relate to doctrine and practice. I wonder what would happen if Saints could find their balance more often and live from a sacred embrace of both being and becoming?

It's my intention to invite an exploration in your own heart, mind, and body around being and becoming. In my experience, there's a place of complete rest, openness, and joy that can hold both of these qualities. You don't have to give up either—you can have it all. It's right here, right now, always available.

Let's explore how you can become perfected, while simultaneously being completely whole.

THE HEART OF THE MESSAGE

This section is the heart of my offering to you, dear reader. If you don't read the whole book, or you want to remember how it all fits, this is the essence of what I want to share:

In every moment of life, we hold an interior sensibility, or orientation, to our experiences:

- **Internal division**: avoidance, rejection, aversion, separateness, or
- **Internal union**: acceptance, openness, unguardedness, full intimacy.

In all moments of life, Christ *starts* from internal union, I believe. As Latter-day Saints, we can learn to "not shrink" from our experiences, living in full embrace of all of life, not an inch away from its continual invitation. It's my experience that this first step—a deep acceptance of what is—can bring forward our fullest agentic capacities.

When we resolve internal divisions, we find there are no bitter cups to avoid in our lives. The world is open for our fullest, most divine engagement. We are free. We experience every moment as continually, already whole. This wholeness forms the context for all our life experiences, a canvas upon which all experiences unfold. We feel saved and glorious already, fully in the rest of the Lord no matter what our internal or external conditions are like.

From this rest of the Lord, anything that needs to happen, can. We can choose to do nothing, or act to improve the moment. Rather than letting our egoic conditioning, which is rooted in personal history or past wounding, lead the way, our highest intentions get to author our experience.

As this rest permeates our being more and more, we realize that it's always been here, never leaves, and cannot ever change. Our trust in God's holding of all of existence clarifies and we begin walking as sacred beings in a sacred world, always.

Among other things, I believe this is what the gospel is trying to teach us. For me, I couldn't taste this reality for decades. Now, I'm continually finding myself opening again and again to its truth. This book contains my field notes of that journey, so far.

PART I: BECOMING AND BEING

We'll take each of these perspectives, being and becoming, separately at first. Then, we'll see how they work together while maintaining their unique gifts.

CHAPTER 1:

THE BECOMING VIEWPOINT

Becoming is all about progressing and developing into better people. The Church has clear maps of how we can do this, eventually becoming as God is. In the standard Plan of Happiness, we find a map that charts how a soul progresses through space and time to an ultimate divine destination. In this chapter, we'll explore the relationship between agency and becoming, how our past affects agency, and how to liberate ourselves into truly free agents as we journey forward in the sacred work of becoming.

Being   Becoming

> *Let's Check In:*
>
> In this section, we'll go deeply into the becoming perspective in an attempt to saturate our understanding with its gifts and limitations. Check in with yourself as you read, noticing where you nod your head in agreement or recognition as well as when you disagree, feel aversion, or are confused. It can be an easy way to sense how much of your way of living is aligned with a becoming sensibility.

THE "STANDARD" PLAN OF HAPPINESS

Most people reading this have familiarity with Latter-day Saint frameworks, so we won't spend much time on it here. When I reference God in this book, I usually mean Heavenly Parents. I've spiced up the beginning and end of the Plan of Happiness a little to fit my personal palate, but essentially, the doctrine around human development from an LDS perspective goes something like this:

1. God is light—All that exists; complete intimacy with all
2. God sees/knows/manifests intelligences from existence (intelligence)
3. God organizes intelligences into spirit bodies that develop (intelligence + spirit)
4. Spirit bodies can choose to come to Earth to inhabit a mortal body to develop even more (intelligence + spirit + mortal body)
5. Mortal bodies die as a part of developing (intelligence + spirit – body)
6. Spirits and bodies are resurrected (intelligence + spirit + perfected body)
7. Divine growth continues into eventual Godhood (perfected intelligence + perfected spirit + perfected body)

8. God is light—All that exists 2.0; complete intimacy with All (the you–God)

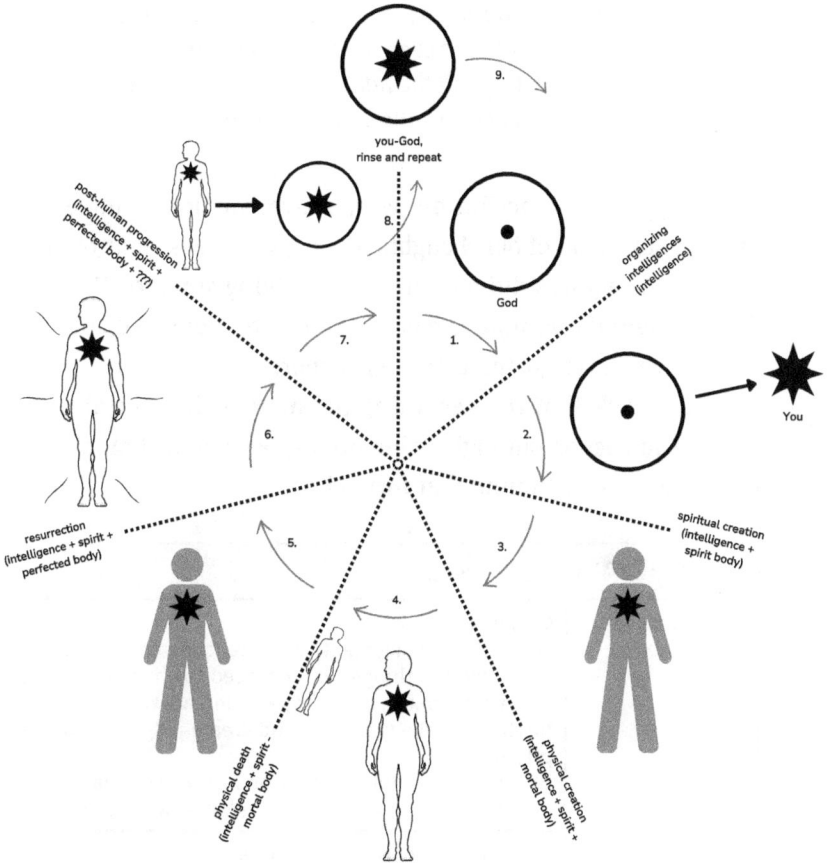

This plan includes lots of becoming. It assumes that we aren't something (gods) currently, and that by doing things, we can become that something (gods). Most of us love filling the measure of our creation—becoming is part of our reason for being on Earth. Latter-day Saint doctrine gives big and small lenses to navigate the process of becoming, including ordinances, authority, age requirements, worthiness/unworthiness, and milestones like baptism, ordinations, missionary service, marriage, and building a family.

"The purpose of the gospel is... to make bad men good and good men better, and to change human nature." -President David O. McKay[1]

"For the natural man is an enemy to God, and has been from the fall of Adam, and will be, forever and ever, unless he yields to the enticings of the Holy Spirit, and putteth off the natural man and becometh a saint through the Atonement of Christ the Lord" -King Benjamin[2]

Clearly, from a becoming perspective, we don't suddenly become holy in all of our thoughts, words, and deeds—our transformation requires diligent effort and divine support. From a developmental (becoming) position, our intentions and actions impact where we go and how we get there.

The **key skill of the becoming perspective** is to be able to develop and act on our highest intentions, beyond the limitations of the egoic conditioning that formed us.

A short reference for **becoming**	
Basic Essence	Changing what is. The ever-changing reality of content and appearances. The view that things can and need to change, based on what we value, need, hope, or intend. We draw distinctions, make meaning, and create judgments and priorities. We see progress through time and work to decrease the distance between what we are and what we hope to be.
Deals With	Changing content/circumstances.
Fruits of balance	Accomplishment, progress, transformation, inspiration, innovation, new horizons, fulfilling the measure of our creation, becoming good and faithful servants. Feeling a wide sense of agency, continually.
Fruits when taken too far	Not-enoughness, discontent, fear, worry, scarcity; we appear haggard, gaunt, resentful.

---

1 President David O. McKay, in the film "Every Member a Missionary," as quoted by Elder Franklin D. Richards in Conference Report, Oct. 1965.

2 Mosiah 3:19

Tendencies when in balance	Using agency to improve ourselves and the world around us, working toward a higher, more divine reality. Increased capacity to face the relative difficulties of life.
Tendencies when taken too far	Running faster than we have strength. Serving or acting from resentment and scarcity.

AGENCY IN OUR TRAJECTORY

In order for us to successfully inhabit the becoming viewpoint, we must believe in free agency. From the becoming perspective, we can sense or see a future possibility and then use our agency to close the gap between our current condition and where we want to end up. It's the idea that something or someone inside of us has an intention and can act in ways to bring that intention about. As a simple example, consider the path of becoming a bodybuilder. Most adults could give a list of five important habits to grow their muscle mass and could imagine themselves doing so. Their plan only breaks down if their agency somehow fails them along the way—maybe they choose to sleep in and miss a workout, eat foods that don't support muscle gain, or lose focus in distraction and other priorities.

See if this is true for yourself. Ask, what's one thing I want to become? Do you have a list of steps to get there? If not, can you use agency to figure out the steps? Once you have your plan, can you follow it? Our becoming power breaks down if our ability to choose is limited.

Agency is about how we show up in the world, every moment, and how that showing up changes the course of our lives. LDS theology holds a sacred place for agency, and teaches that consequences on the becoming path return directly to the agent:

"Be not deceived; God is not mocked: for whatsoever a man soweth, that shall he also reap." Galatians 6:7

You get out what you put in. While the heart of this message is true, in my experience, agency is actually much more complicated than a black and white explanation around sowing and reaping.

Where does agency start? Where does it stop? Can I choose my thoughts, feelings, and actions? Can God judge me for something I can't choose? (I personally don't think we are judged for things outside of our choice, like Adam's transgression.[3]) So where is that line? Is it a line?

- Will I be judged for the weather today? *No, of course not.*
- What about how I feel about the weather? *Well, maybe.*
- What about if I don't plan well and leave my rain jacket at home and then I'm full of hatred on my bike coming home from work? Then when I see my family, I'm a real grinch? *This is complicated...*

Assuming that God doesn't judge us for things outside our agency, it seems really important to know where our agency starts and stops. For one, clarifying the boundaries of agency can relieve guilt and shame, which opens up our sense of agency again. Or, it can bring healthy remorse back online, which can realign our intentions and mental maps with reality.

We often judge ourselves for things that are outside our conscious control, including things like random thoughts, bodily reactions, dreams, or even desires. We put too much on ourselves.

Other times, we don't take accountability for something in our sphere that we actually can impact through our agency. We short-change ourselves, thinking the world is much smaller than it actually is! We can become victims of the moment, a thing to be acted upon, with no idea how to act as an agent again.[4]

Like a saint holding to the Iron Rod, it's important that our grip is not too tight, and not too loose. If we hold too tightly to the rod, the clenching of our hand on the rod actually impedes us from walking toward the Tree of Life—there's too much friction.

3 Article of Faith 2

4 Hymn 131

At the same time, holding too loosely can detach us from the Word, leaving us disconnected from a potentially helpful source.

Likewise, if we blame ourselves for everything, and beat ourselves up, that's holding too tightly. If we say we have no influence over any of our thoughts, words, actions, desires, and such, that's probably holding too loosely. Both extremes leave us with an unhelpful experience of agency. Understanding agency more deeply can increase our capacity to engage in our becoming from our Highest Self.

HOW THE PAST AFFECTS AGENCY

"Wherefore, men are free according to the flesh; and all things are given them which are expedient unto man. And they are free to choose liberty and eternal life." D&C 58:27–28

Again, when I hear a scripture like this, it makes it sound so easy. Free according to the flesh? Choose liberty and eternal life? Cool, let's do it. But, when it comes down to the moment-by-moment experience of agency, it becomes much more complicated, more nuanced. In the spirit of everything "virtuous, lovely, or of good report or praiseworthy,"[5] let's look at how some Western psychologists understand agency.

Psychologists have mapped biological patterns of self-preservation that unconsciously and consciously guide our actions. Our bodies internally function without our agency all the time, including breathing, heart beating, digesting, renewing cells, and regulating our immune system. The body also monitors an external world via perceptions like sounds, images, and sensations. Yet, we're only consciously aware of a small fraction of

---

5 Article of Faith 13

what's being picked up by our senses. Something unconscious is managing every moment of our experience, usually optimizing for our safety, love, and care.

Most humans are born with a set of automatic reactions, including pulling your hand away from a hot stove, noticing fast moving objects in your peripheral vision, and recoiling if you look down and see a dark shape coiled up in front of you. It's the "base set" of automatic reactions that benefit every human by increasing their chances of surviving. We don't usually "have agency," per se, over these reactions.

Trigger	Your Automatic Reaction
Extreme heat on skin, burn	Near-instant somatic contraction reflex
Dropping something precious	Core contracts to support a limb extending to catch object
Seeing dark thin shape coiled in front of you	Eyes widen, breath catches, arms go out to halt movement
Fast-moving object in peripheral vision	Head turns, eyes locate, breath catches
Plunge into cold water	Gasping, decreased cerebral blood perfusion, spike in stress hormones
Inner nose tickle	Sneeze
Touch baby's corner of mouth; touch roof of mouth	Rooting reflex; sucking reflex

One way we might lose our agency occurs before the age of accountability, even as infants. In addition to this "base set," there's another set of automatic responses (again, outside of agency) that start building up in our biology based on the life experiences we have. This new set impacts our neural network, muscle responses, and even what perceptions our brain will *let us* be aware of. That's right—we have unconscious filters between us and the world. The "base set" of automaticity gets updated by our *specific life conditions* to optimize for physical, mental, and social well-being.[6]

For example, sometimes as children we'll have a reaction to something and emote or act out. Our caregivers, teachers, or church leaders may not know how to respond to us and inadvertently remove their safety, love, and care from us. This sends a direct signal to our unconscious operation manual to make a note about the thing (usually our emotions or actions) that led to the removal of adult safety, love, and care. From there on out, especially if that pattern repeats, our system will internally hinder our ability to allow that inside feeling, thought, or action to emerge into our awareness or behavior.[7]

For example, if I expressed my emotional pain as a child by crying and yelling, but my parents shut me down and removed their care of me, I would (unconsciously) learn that feeling and expressing pain is not conducive to my survival, and my survival system would divorce myself internally from those feelings and expressions, even though they naturally arise.[8] I would eventually orphan off whole aspects of my lived experience, creating patterns of dividing myself from what's actually here in my embodied experience. I'm in pain and I know it on some level, but I also know I can't feel it or express it. I become increasingly divided from my real experience of life.

---

6 Dr. Stephen Porges' 2004 study on subconscious threat detection states, "Polyvagal Theory proposes that the neural evaluation of risk and safety reflexively triggers shifts in autonomic state without requiring conscious awareness. Thus, the term "neuroception" was introduced to emphasize a neural process, distinct from perception, capable of distinguishing environmental and visceral features that are safe, dangerous, or life-threatening." Also see Paul Ekman's *Emotions Revealed* for more on "auto-appraisers," which are the processes governing pre-conscious nervous system decision-making.

7 Dr. Gabor Maté frames this as the unconscious childhood preference for Acceptance rather than Authenticity in expressing our internal experience, because we have to choose our basic needs being met over choosing our emotions and going without the basics. See *The Myth of Normal.*

8 This removal of parental care sometimes happens on overt levels, including physical neglect or leaving the room, but it can also happen on subtle levels, like the parent's face going flat, giving the child dead eyes, a stern look, or simply becoming quiet, distant, and unavailable to the child.

As a child, I'm in an impossible situation—do I distance myself *from my own pain* to keep my parents close? Or do I risk distancing myself *from my own parents* to keep my pain close (meaning I'm aware of it, feeling it, expressing it)? Which do I choose? Since we can't put on a suit and a tie and set up interviews for new parents, physically staying in the situation is our only real choice. Our survival-oriented mind and body choose for us, and we begin distancing ourselves from more and more of our normal, internal experiences in order to prioritize caregiver acceptance. It works—we stay physically alive.[9]

With each experience like this, our internal survival intelligence adds more automatic reactions to our base set.[10] These responses weren't with us at birth, but are learned socially in order to maximize acceptance from caregivers and our community. Here are a few made-up examples:

Trigger	Your Automatic Reaction
Stern voice tone	Face goes flaccid, eyes widen, external awareness increases
Silence from loved one	Heaviness in chest, feeling of hopelessness
Parent's jaw tightens	Breath catches, body pulls away, heart rate increases
Loved one's gaze falls to the ground	Face flushes, brow furrows, knot in stomach
Parent sighs and shakes head at you	Internal sensation of collapse, heaviness in head, numbness in limbs, fatigue

---

9 Sadly, these internal scripts can also influence how we understand God, even to the point of creating a dynamic of always trying to be acceptable to Heavenly Parents out of a primal fear that we'll be annihilated if we aren't thinking, feeling, believing, or acting appropriately. When we bring childhood frames into our spirituality, we severely limit the kind of meaningful relationship with the Sacred we can develop. As we'll see shortly from an adult consciousness, Heavenly Parents—and our participation in the womb of all creation—can begin to take on new shapes.

10 Please note that not everyone experiences this kind of developmental conditioning or trauma (which can range from mild to extreme). Your exact automatic reactions most likely differ from the list, as each person's nature interacts uniquely with how they are nurtured. I also firmly believe that parents are doing their best. I personally find parenting to be one of the hardest things I've ever done.

Authority figure corrects you	Intense burning in chest, throat, hands; urge to stomp, yell, or leave
Parent keeps talking about themselves	Feeling alone, sensations of numbness and sinking

These experiences really take hold the first couple decades of life, after which they solidify into ways of daily living, and then often go untouched after that. (Again, your exact map of internal reactions will be different; these are just examples.) Even though our life context changes and our adult capacities come online, we still automatically reference these old maps of behavior in our adult lives. This may mean that I, as a husband, cannot express my emotional pain in front of my wife because of a learned pattern as a child, even though I'm in an entirely new context with completely new people responding to me.

Most of us aren't aware of the internal automatic reaction we're having, so we're just living life from heaviness, hopelessness, or tension. And, we've learned through sad experience that if we try to express those sensations in a relational dynamic, our felt sense of acceptance goes down. So, we continually distance ourselves, internally, from a very foundational ground (somatic sensation) of our experience. Instead of using our immediate, embodied experience, we take our old reactivity maps as the default setting in every moment.

AGENCY RIGHT HERE AND NOW

The becoming skill is a freedom to act on our highest intentions, yet if old scripts are guiding our experience, how can we truly be free to become what we want to be? We can see the path ahead of us, yet we find there are invisible blocks that halt our progress along the path of transformation. We need to be liberated from these blocks in order to take necessary action on our path. So let's get back to agency—if I have an internal, unconscious script that tells me I cannot feel or express pain, where's my ability to choose? It's as if our agency is mostly pristine on Day 1, and then life updates it from there on out, optimizing initially for safety, love, and care.[11] Early life often gives us a new template of what can and cannot happen in our internal experience, and it's often so unconscious that most people deny they have any of these sorts of restrictions, claiming that all people can do what they really want, if they really, really want it, simply by "trying harder."[12]

The trouble with trying harder, when it comes to unconscious stuckness, is that it doesn't work, in my experience. And, sometimes the violence we commit against ourselves—in the process of trying to force our system to do something that it's written strict codes against doing—isn't worth the outcome.

I'm going to invite a real-time exploration. It's playful and fun, and very informative. See if you can roll with it.

Welcome to a three-minute agency exercise: just lie down on the floor on your back, like you're an infant, and giggle and laugh and kick your legs a few times. Loll your tongue around, slobber a little, and roll your eyes. Make nonsense noise. Be loud, sad, joyful, angry, and cute.

How'd that go? Did you actually try it? It only takes three minutes. If you tried it, notice what that was like for you. Maybe even write down some impressions in a journal.

If you didn't try it, why not? You're a free agent, right? So you are free to choose to do this. And to choose not to do it. Think about why you did or didn't. Write down the reasons for your choice. If you didn't do it, was it because you're in a public setting? So what! You're free to choose. Or maybe an awkward feeling came up when you thought about lying flat on the bus

---

11 Note that there are probably many other ways that we gain and lose agency in the course of human life. The unique advantages and disadvantages of our early years are just one angle to examine here, chosen because of my clinical experience and personal feedback regarding its high leverage capacity to transform us.

12 For a beautiful exploration on this topic, check out Aundi Kolber, *Try Softer: A Fresh Approach to Move Us out of Anxiety, Stress, and Survival Mode—and into a Life of Connection and Joy.*

floor on the way to work? Even if you didn't choose for that awkward feeling to happen, can't you choose to ignore it and do the exercise anyway?

Did you not do it because you don't have time? Well, you're reading this right now, so you could just do it right now. Go ahead. Or was it because you simply didn't want to (and still don't)? If you're a free agent, can't you choose what you want? Who chose that you didn't want to do it? Aren't you in charge?

Maybe you realize you can't choose every feeling that comes up for you, or even your desires, but that you can only *respond* to these. Okay, so go ahead and do the exercise now, even if you don't want to, or if it feels awkward. Or maybe you're saying that it just doesn't align with your values as a human, and you only act in ways that align with your values. Nice! Did you choose your values? What if you just add this three-minute exercise to your values right now? I know that's somewhat silly. I promise it won't harm you.

When I was first asked to do this exercise, it was in a group setting, and everyone was trying it.[13] But, I just couldn't do it! Honestly, it felt so strange to me. I kept looking at other people and I felt really embarrassed. They told me that this was so easy—it's something even a baby can do, but I felt so tensed up about it. I tried to talk myself into doing it or change my feelings around it. No matter how hard I tried, something visceral inside me seemed to prevent me from doing it, despite my intentions.

This actually felt like something important for me to learn, so I went home and practiced almost every day for a month. Sometimes it was when I'd wake up in the middle of the night, and I'd stare up at the ceiling and let myself remember my infant self, fully in the world, without intention and without distinction from anything in the moment.

Eventually, I felt more at ease with letting my body engage in these movements, sounds, and sensations. It's like I reclaimed some old part of me, and more than anything, I felt that I got

---

13 Thank you, GTC 22.

my body back. Before this exercise, I was quite self-conscious about my body in movement—dancing, being expressive, improv games, etc. And somehow this exercise released that. It got me back into organic, intuitive movement that has been a real blessing since then.

Please feel my intention in my words: I believe that doing little experiments like this can really open us up more deeply to the moment, reveal the true nature of agency, and ultimately liberate us into more compassionate beings.

Chances are that you can find some edge to what we consider agency. In the cluster of sensations, thoughts, images, and feelings you had during the doing or not doing of the exercise, which portions did you "choose"? Most people don't like the idea that there are limitations to what they can choose. But, in my experience, the reality is right in front of us most of the time: We aren't actually as free as we claim. Even a simple three-minute exercise that requires no skills at all can seem literally impossible to us, and the reasons we give about why we can't do it ultimately boil down to "I don't want to," which is totally fair. When prompted to use our agency and just "choose to want to," we correctly conclude "I just can't," or we just say "no."

This reality, "I just can't," is where these unconscious maps of our early training truly reveal themselves. Whenever you know what you want to do, or intend to do, but you just can't, chances are that there's an unseen rule that your body or mind is holding with the intention to keep you safe. However, as we stated before, these rules are often decades old, based on data that happened when you were a child in a completely different context. The rules don't apply the same way to your adult life now, but your system hasn't been updated since then, when you were so sponge-like. There's a chance you hardened up before adulthood, crusting into the shape of those formative years, and now you may sometimes use childhood lessons and logic to live life in completely new settings and contexts.

For a simple exercise like the one I suggested, it's not too bad if you can't do it, even when you try really hard. But what if the task is overcoming an addiction? Or having a conversation that feels impossible? Coming out to your parents? Facing your depression? Parenting a child that drives you absolutely crazy?

It can feel so overwhelming and impossible to make significant change when we're fighting unconscious stuckness. It's easy to beat ourselves up, blame our character or willpower, or actually decide something negative about our worth as a person. However, it seems so obvious to me that God knows it's more complex than that: "for the Lord seeth not as man seeth; for man looketh on the outward appearance, but the Lord looketh on the heart."[14]

If you're the kind of person who easily gets down on yourself (as humankind so often does), try not seeing yourself as harshly as you usually do. Bring some trust and compassion that there's probably more going on in your "failures" than you simply "not trying hard enough." It's my experience that, paradoxically, softening up the tight hold on believing we have complete "free agency" over our thoughts, feelings, desires, and capacities is helpful in uncovering a deeper sense of agency.

AN OPEN CITY

One metaphor that has been helpful to me is imagining my life as a dense city. Think Chicago, Paris, or New York. When I'm born, all roads are open, equal, and available for me to drive or bike down. But, starting as a kid, I go through life traveling these roads, and from time to time have bad experiences down some of them. I might crash on one road, or get hit with indigestion and intestinal gas down one, or get mugged, or smell something

---

14 1 Samuel 16:7

weird, or get hit by a rainstorm down another. These experiences are the physical and emotional difficulties we run into.

When anything like this happens, some part of me wants to protect me, and so it rules out that street forevermore—off limits! Pretty soon, more and more streets get blocked off, and when I want to go somewhere that requires that route, I get to the street and see big signs, road blocks, and scary warnings (our protective internal sensations). I pull away from the shortest path to my destination and have to re-route, still getting close to my endpoint eventually, but having to take the long way around.

The more I live, the more I find roads that are closed. My capacity for riding down a street with basically *anything* unpleasant has disappeared, and now I begin planning routes as if the closed roads weren't ever options. Some part of me completely forgets that those avenues were once open and convenient to the task at hand. And I ride around town in the strangest of ways to get somewhere that's just around the corner.

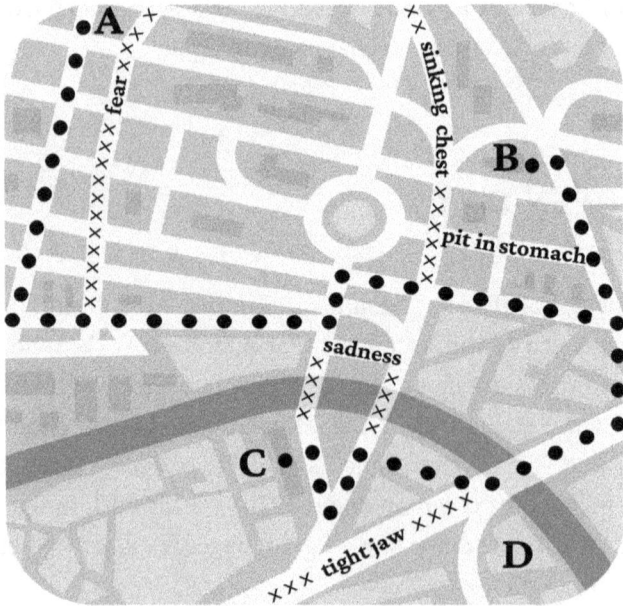

Eventually, New York City feels really small and inconvenient. Getting from A to B is a headache. It doesn't actually matter where I have to go; I just hate traveling, and everything and everyone seems to bug me. Any destination is a complete inconvenience and I begin complaining about how the city is set up.

My life becomes small. Simple actions and tasks seem impossible. Everything around me is just one more reason to loathe myself and my life circumstances. All moments feel like a demand on energy I just don't have. My strategies aren't working. I obviously cannot keep living this way.

One day I read something or talk to someone who describes going down a "forbidden, closed" street on my map. I tell them *That's impossible!* Yet, they convince me the street is still open. I'm not positive I could travel that road myself, but I'm curious, so I follow them to the road.

There, they walk past the warning signs and keep going. They don't shrink away. I shout that we have to turn back, but they give me some support when it gets scary. I don't make it all the way through, but even going halfway (and not dying) feels like a revelation. I hate the experience and love it at the same time. What could this mean? Is there actually a way out of miserable New York?

My new mentor and I begin going on daily rides and walks further and further down scary, stinky, traumatic, stormy, and cobwebbed streets. It turns out that over half of them are actually not scary at all, now that I'm an adult. They just looked scary from my crusted-over kid perspective.

Some of them are genuinely terrifying, though. Those are the ones that I still squint my eyes during, then pant like a dog once I'm through. But eventually, even those roads seem passable—accessible again to my GPS mapping.

Soon, I begin realizing that my everyday life is really full of disturbances—bad smells, annoying people, and the wrong weather. They're everywhere! But my stamina and threshold for dealing with them have increased. I get places faster, can pursue what I'm passionate about more easily, and begin liking the city again. I realize that my previous way of being, where I avoided everything potentially uncomfortable, was also an unsatisfying way to live. So, at the end of the day, if it's upsetting to drive down the scary streets *and* upsetting to have to avoid them all the time, why not just pick the life that feels more open?

From this vantage point, I can visit any destination via any path. Rather than my fear being in control, now my heart's desires begin to lead. Infinite possibilities for what has been and can be are emerging every day.

All roads are open. Discomfort is part of my life, but it's not calling the shots. My adult self moves and grooves from its most generous self. Agency is back in business. I can finally buy the "I heart NYC" shirt. And I actually mean it.

INPUTS AND OUTPUTS

If the narrative and metaphor formats aren't helpful for you in understanding how agency is impacted by our nature and nurture, consider a more mechanical diagram (see next page).

As you can see, the outputs are directly impacted by how the inputs are interpreted. So if we want to understand why our outputs are so good or bad, we really have to understand *how* inputs are handled.

This can get a bit too mechanistic quickly, so I want to be clear that I don't experience myself or others as simple input and output machines, but it's been a helpful metaphor for myself and others in understanding this part of the agency experience.

We sometimes experience ourselves as these lasting, solid, separate entities in the world. We guess that we can have *purely objective* inputs and outputs. In some ways that can be helpful, and at the same time we begin to learn that we are constantly in the jelly thickness of continual inputs from our environment. We're never really separate in our observation of a thing, but rather we're always an observer-in-the-observed. Inputs swirl around and in us, they go through our filters of meaning-making, and then give us our list of potential outputs. This happens incredibly fast.

As much as we like to believe the contrary, our perception of the world isn't often very clear. Any inputs we get from the world—which for many of us are just sensory perceptions like hearing, feeling, seeing—are put through our filters. As mentioned previously, these filters have both genetic and learned origins, but the result is similar: Our automatic meaning-making is actually determining what we can experience after the inputs are unconsciously appraised, filtered, and then selectively revealed to us.

Let's say I'm checking the balances in my bank accounts (inputs) while at a stop light coming home from work, and I have a history of financial instability and struggle (internal meaning-making and filters based on past experiences). Those inputs

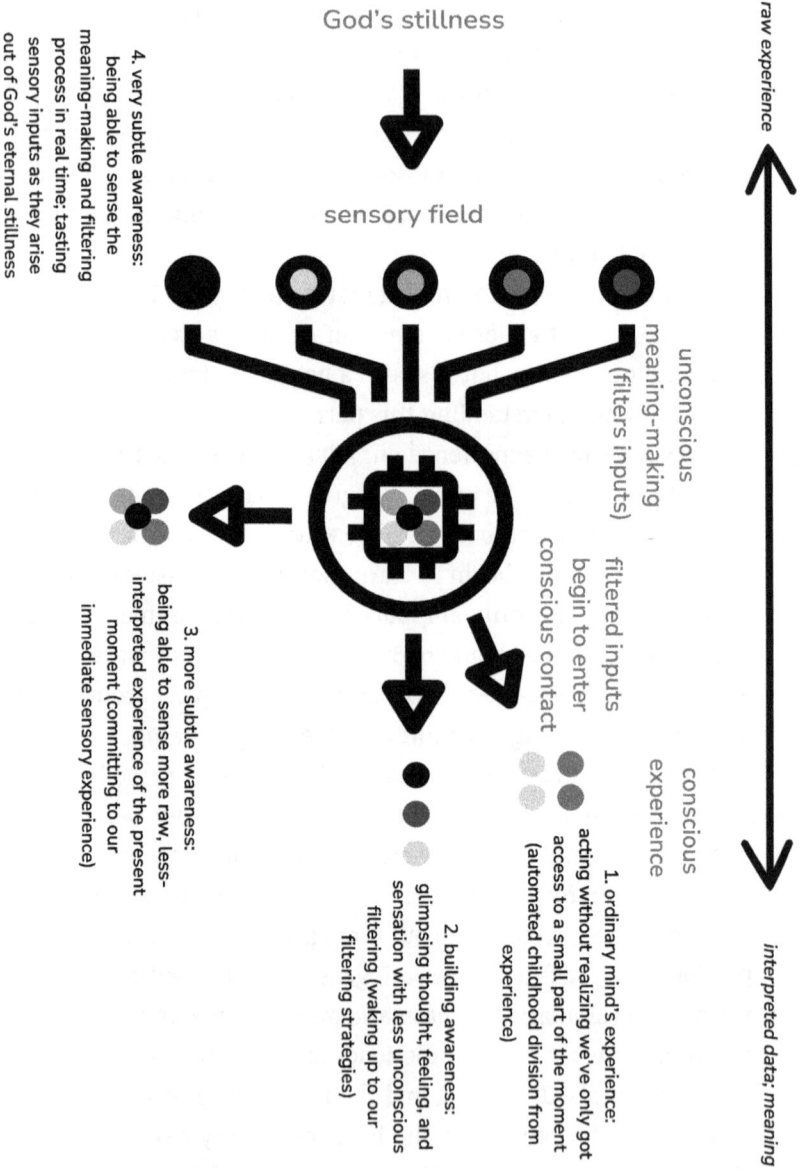

God's stillness

sensory field

raw experience

interpreted data; meaning

unconscious meaning-making (filters inputs)

filtered inputs begin to enter conscious contact

conscious experience

4. very subtle awareness: being able to sense the meaning-making and filtering process in real time; tasting sensory inputs as they arise out of God's eternal stillness

3. more subtle awareness: being able to sense more raw, less-interpreted experience of the present moment (committing to our immediate sensory experience)

1. ordinary mind's experience: acting without realizing we've only got access to a small part of the moment (automated childhood division from experience)

2. building awareness: glimpsing thought, feeling, and sensation with less unconscious filtering (waking up to our filtering strategies)

(bank balances) into my system will be interpreted a certain way. Their interpretation will then guide what responses (outputs of sensations, feelings, thoughts, ideas) I can naturally have. Certain responses seem accessible (feeling tension or stress, wanting to scold my wife for buying "too many school supplies," beating myself up for that impulse buy yesterday, etc.) while other responses seem impossible or completely off the radar (feeling ease and lightness in my chest, expressing gratitude to my wife for all her beautiful intentions and work that day, holding compassion and love for myself).

Some parts of this process feel intuitively like agency, where I can intervene and change the moment. Others seem to happen automatically and before my intentions can kick in. This is frequently the case for most people I know, including myself. Only after I learned about more and more refined levels of meaning-making and body-mind systems and then tested these in my own experience of agency, did I realize how incomplete my sense of free agency was. Of course, it's still evolving, but I'm delighted with the fruits of learning the inputs and outputs dynamic related to agency.

In my experience, the work of becoming is reborn when we unveil what unconscious, automatic data interpretation is happening so that we can begin calibrating toward our highest intentions, instead of maintaining our childhood calibration of staying acceptable to our caregivers at all costs.

BECOMING FREE AGENTS

A deeper sense of free agency comes when we can uncover all the hidden rules, maps, and "shoulds" that guide our pre-conscious experience. Doing this requires lots of tough work, because it requires going against the fundamental rule set that our system currently uses.

Going back to our example of not being able to feel emotional pain as a child, if the mind-body system has a strong biological momentum against letting our pain be felt internally or expressed externally, doing those things will have intense effects. Changing the shape of a dry, crusty sponge is much more intense than a warm, soft, wet sponge. In many ways, the intention is to get back to that supple, flexible, adaptable version of ourselves that was impressionable and sensitive, but this time those qualities will be paired with a mature adult's sensibilities. Instead of acting out of historical habit, we act from the moment freshly and become more helpful to the demands of the moment.

When our internal rules solidify, they often lock the door to the control room by using intense sensations. Put another way, when you start heading into "forbidden territory," your body will light up with very intense sensations as a way to ward you off. Notice, the intense sensations aren't about right and wrong, they're about historically-informed pain rules. "Don't cry in front of dad" isn't actually a moral claim, it's simply the wisest conclusion a young mind can make to keep itself as safe as possible.

To reclaim a deeper sense of agency, we need to enter the territories of the soul, and most importantly *the body*, that were previously off limits. We can acclimate the mind and body to new sensations, thoughts, feelings, and beliefs to expand the borders of what we deem "okay to do." To clarify the intention and direction here, I believe that our truest sense of agency comes when we can fully reside in an openness of choice—I can cry right now, or not. I can serve, or not serve. I can be alone, or be together. I can be loud, I can be soft. Some have called this place of infinite possibility a Still Point.[15]

Someone who resides at a Still Point has a sense of liberation, where the tug to do one thing or another doesn't come from past limitations, nor does it come from "shoulds" or from a sense of

---

15 John Kesler, *Integral Polarity Practice in Service of Leadership for Flourishing.*

not-enoughness. The intention to act in ways appropriate to the moment comes from the deepest virtue of the Divine inside, an open and infinite source of inexhaustible goodness.

The response, "I just can't," disappears. Barriers to what's possible fall away. Both sides of a choice illuminate themselves before us and we have a deep sense of clarity to see what's needed in the moment, for the greatest good of the moment. We can also choose not to engage. This, to me, feels like a more expansive, uninhibited agency.

So how do we get from where we currently are—automatically carrying out obsolete, limiting childhood patterns—to truly living from the becoming perspective—acting on and fulfilling our highest intentions with as little limitation as possible? There are dozens of effective ways, ranging from psychotherapy, spiritual practices, journaling, physical transformations and release, and meditative practices. In fact, most spiritual traditions have some sort of map you can follow that will lead you to their version of "free to choose."

From an LDS perspective, the Atonement of Jesus Christ is at the heart of these transformations. Tapping into an infinite source of forgiveness, power, and support allows humankind to become more than their past, more than their upbringing. Let's try a short exercise:

Take a moment to find a feeling or a thought that makes you uncomfortable. Examples may include:

Feeling of loss or sorrow
Feeling anger or resentment
Thinking "I'm not good enough"
Thinking "Others can be forgiven, but I can't get over those past sins"

Now, let that thought or feeling just be there, and begin to explore what's happening in the body. If you have practiced body awareness, you'll immediately find a wealth of information—tension, heaviness, heat, swirling, bracing, pulling, etc. If you haven't practiced body awareness, you may have trouble locating something right away. If that's the case for you, try this out:

What's active right now?
Do you feel it the most in your head, chest, or stomach?
In that place, is it tight or loose? Heavy or light? Big or small?
That should be enough information to do the exercise—you don't have to find much more.

From here, notice if you like or don't like feeling these sensations. Most of us don't, and we do things to avoid feeling the sensations. We're going to do the opposite here. Let yourself, on purpose, feel exactly what's happening through the body. You may find that all of you wants to pull away from it, and that's where the Atonement can be helpful for Latter-day Saints.

Set a timer for 60 seconds; that's all you need to feel this thing and then we'll be done. If it's helpful, imagine Jesus standing next to you, or hugging you as you feel this intensity. Imagine a blanket of His light or love shimmering around you to create a container in which to feel the intensity. Let yourself give in to all the intensity of the sensations (they won't damage you). Truly, let the sensations in your body fully have you, let them have their way with all of you, swirling-shifting-growing-shrinking-expanding-contracting, for just 60 seconds. With God, all things are possible.

Okay, after 60 seconds, shake that off. Breathe. Relax, reset, and come back to feeling Earth's gravity and the ground beneath your feet and seat.

Feel free to make a few notes, or just let whatever happened, and didn't happen, settle.

NOT SHRINKING

What you just did is something Christ mastered. He had an enormous, even divine, capacity not to shrink in the face of intensity. There were many bitter cups that were put in front of Him, but something about his relationship to intensity of experience allowed him to drink them all. I personally believe that He embodies our truest sense of agency, where no experience is innately too much for us. *The ability not to shrink, or to shrink, is true agency.* When one side of a choice isn't available, that's not free agency. Both poles must be open for choice to exist. Most of us get stuck in *shrinking*, understandably, and *not shrinking* is closed to us.

As we know, a house divided cannot stand. This is true for external things like churches and families, but also for our internal world. Are there any divisions within you? Places where you've blocked or restricted access, where you're divided from yourself and your experience? Do you shrink from your own sensations, feelings, thoughts? It's my experience that opening ourselves to the ultimate intensities of our immediate, embodied experience is one beautiful way to unify the internal house.

What if there were no rooms of your soul you couldn't enter? What if no memory, thought, belief, feeling, or sensation required you to turn away? What if, instead, you could hold that bitter cup with all the confidence, love, warmth, and trust of a god, and choose what was best, instead of shrinking from what you "just couldn't do."

As you can sense, pretty soon along this path, our entire orientation to choice and life shifts. Before, we often made choices based on which bitter cups we couldn't drink. But when we have the divine capacity to drink any cup at any time for any reason, avoiding bitterness no longer becomes a criterion for our choices.

Remember, bitter cups can be physical actions, but at a more refined level are intense internal thoughts, feelings, and sensations. Even beyond that, there are more refined layers of resistance or distancing from full, unguarded openness to immediate experience. I think Christ had this complete trust to be open to life. Even in His anger, His grief, His joy, His anguish, I imagine that if I looked into His eyes, the full disturbance of His feeling would still be present, but backgrounded by something eternal that never tarnishes. In those eternal eyes, I think I would sense Him still, and always, in the rest of the Lord. As we'll see in the next chapter, I think this rest is what allowed Him to go further than ever into disturbance.[16]

In short, as Christ showed, avoidance of difficulty is no longer at the decision-making table. All roads are open. And since all roads are open, we can begin making all of life's choices based on new criteria, and in my opinion, more divine criteria. We begin living life from our highest sense of self, our holiest intentions, our most divine light.

Again, it's worth emphasizing—I believe this is what Christ was doing. With access to infinite power to withstand intensity, He never had to shy away from the moment, internally or externally, and instead was fully open to the blast of life coursing through him and others. And then He was able to act in ways aligned with His highest intentions, regardless of the price, social judgment, pain, discomfort, improbability, or intensity.

In my experience, this is one way we can become free agents.

THE SACRED WORK OF BECOMING

Becoming something divine is a sacred work. You may look at yourself and say, "I don't know if I can really hold that much intensity, or be up to the big tasks of my life." At your current

---

16 When I use the word disturbance, I generally mean intense experience, usually based on body sensations. Disturbance certainly happens emotionally and spiritually as well, but for our purposes here in being and becoming, I find sensation-level disturbance to be most important.

state, that may seem impossible. Much like the new missionary who shows up at the MTC and says, "There's no way I'll ever learn Finnish," you might already have decided what your limits are. Just let that go. If it were you on your own, sure—keep the limitations around. But tethered to an infinite power source, it may be a little too early to decide what you can and cannot become.

The sacred work of becoming includes resolving all internal divisions. Zion is one heart and one mind,[17] and achieving that starts close in,[18] toward the inner chambers of your own heart and mind. Here's a lineup that may describe how you will evolve in your own resolution of dividedness, taken from a master of these arts:[19]

First: Awareness or Recognition
We begin noticing our unconscious strategies that make us shrink from our own internal experience. We may begin seeing a powerful avoidant momentum throughout our life and see the large price we are paying for it. We can realize that our limitations in life have a foundation in our fundamental aversion to the internal experiences we cannot tolerate.

Second: Tolerating
We can begin allowing ourselves to feel our worst fears, realizing that feeling them won't kill us or damage us. We stop trying to abolish them, but instead build a new relationship with them, slowly and surely building capacity and resilience in feeling them.

Third: Acceptance
We find a more open acceptance of when our core vulnerabilities and extreme discomforts come up. We can say yes to feeling more and more, realizing that these experiences are simply part of us,

---

17 Moses 7:18

18 David Whyte, "Start Close In"

19 Bruce Tift, *Already Free: Buddhism Meets Psychotherapy on the Path of Liberation*. I've been deeply influenced by this man's work, and trying to apply what he emulates was a leading inspiration in starting this book.

and therefore we're saying yes to ourselves, the whole house that is us, in a deeper way.

Fourth: Being Kind

We actually begin to be kind to our fears, moving toward that disturbance with warmth. This is where we really tap into our mature adult and divine capacities instead of immature child capacities, so we can reconnect to ourselves with compassion and kindness.

Fifth: Welcoming

We can begin to invite intensity or disturbance without fear or needing it to find us first. We realize that internal disturbance is a chance to look deeper into ourselves, finding sacred moments in disturbance.

Sixth: Committing Completely

We have no reservations, no ounce of avoidance, no backing away from any moment, any part, any feeling that comes into our experience. We are fully available to our immediate, embodied experience, continually. We release any subtle hope that all this work will actually lead to disturbances ever going away, and we fully commit to a life and eternity with sensory disturbance. We find less and less to protect and defend against, resting openly to life more consistently.

Seventh: Loving

We actually love our worst fears and vulnerabilities, not just as an idea, but from our deepest and most sacred heart. We hold experience much like we'd soothe a crying infant, giving perfect love no matter the condition or intensity of the moment. Internal division dissolves completely. We give up abandoning ourselves, never leaving the truth of our immediate and embodied experience. We become a walking Zion microcosm, at one with all of creation.

If you ever meet someone who lives in the last few stages of this list, the power is palpable. In my experience, there are often a handful (or more) of men and women in our communities who live from this place consistently. In his book, Bruce Tift says it this way:

"At this point, we may experience a significant shift in our sense of self: we may realize that what's always there is the activity of kindness. Regardless of whether we like or dislike what arises in our experience, we have become most reliably the activity of kindness."[20]

This is the mind of Christ, for me. And He's much more, of course. But this quality of infinite kindness, of never turning away, is for all of us. It's truly good news. We learn to trust an everlasting kindness that is first given to us,[21] and then begins to be our baseline. Our resting heart rate becomes one of unqualified kindness to all of manifestation—the living Earth world, the world of thoughts and emotions, and the realms of our awareness.[22] Resolving internal divisions requires more and more trust in God the further you move down the list. Eventually, the compulsive need to fix ourselves drops—there's no distance from us and our dangerous, "devilish, carnal" self, no need to live an arm's length away from ourselves, and we feel more confident, embodied, openhearted, present, and engaged.

At this point, agency feels different. The world is open wide. All paths are open. We are liberated. Our very subtle withholding from ourselves leaves, allowing us to also open wholly, unitedly, to God. Because "the Lord requireth the heart and a willing mind,"[23] we now become a vessel for a more potent spiritual field.

I also want to mention at this point that (if we're typically-conditioned Latter-day Saints), when we see a list like this,

---

20 Bruce Tift, *Already Free*, 54.

21 1 John 4:19.

22 3 Nephi 22: 10; D&C 133:52; My Kindness Shall Not Depart From Thee, Rob Gardner.

23 D&C 64:34

we might find ourselves judging ourselves and deciding that we shouldn't be where we're at. We have trouble accepting our place on the journey, feel a lack, and feel an urge to become something different. So, just see where you're at. In fact, let's make it multiple-choice:[24]

A) Oh great, one more place I'm getting it wrong! I'm so ashamed.

B) Well, looks like I've got work to do. I better start immediately.

C) This probably doesn't apply to me.

D) It looks like each phase is so important and I can see where I'm at. I'm OK with that. I know it's not connected to ultimate worth.

Again, there is a sensibility of the mind and heart that actually fully believes and feels that every stage of our development is beautiful, sacred, and holy. But, it's so hard for us to actually feel it and believe it, usually because of lots of conditioning and baggage from our past. Just be gentle with yourself here, and know that you're whole right now, and will be tomorrow, and will be in ten years... and you'll be changing the entire time. This is often where the being perspective is very helpful, as we'll soon explore.

LIMITATIONS OF THE BECOMING PERSPECTIVE

Before moving on, here's a short comment about how becoming can run us in the wrong direction. As you saw with our potential reaction to the previous list, becoming can quickly spin us out if it's not balanced and held appropriately. In my experience, church meetings and activities honor our need to change, but rarely let up on the feeling that *we are fallen in nature and working hard not*

---

24 Another fun way to do this multiple choice test is based on your body. Check in and see what you sense as you read:

A) So tight, contracted stomach and chest, flooded and scattered mind.

B) Heaviness in the chest, eyes are downcast, face is flaccid.

C) Numb, floaty, blank.

D) Open chest, settled stomach and pelvic muscles, shoulders and face relaxed.

to be. In some sense, there's a fundamental aversion to the other side, *that we are also divine*, always. Even now. And now. And now.

We can take a seven-stage list much too far and begin to turn against ourselves. Sometimes we even use our self-antagonism to try to fuel our development, thinking that it's worth hurting ourselves forward into a later stage. In this sense, the becoming energy of church engagement is often saturated with a taste of "not enough." The fact that we're supposed to be perfect but can't be, means we're always behind, always could do more, always not there.

Sometimes the Sacred Work of becoming can feel like the "Never-Ending-Fix-Me-Work" of becoming. It's discouraging, incomplete, unsatisfying, and truly feels never-ending. This is the limitation of only holding the becoming viewpoint. Church members can fill meetings and books, and even the rest of eternity, with this idea that we'll always be improving. That's beautiful. And, we can also unintentionally create a fundamental aversion to what is here, right now, in its beauty.

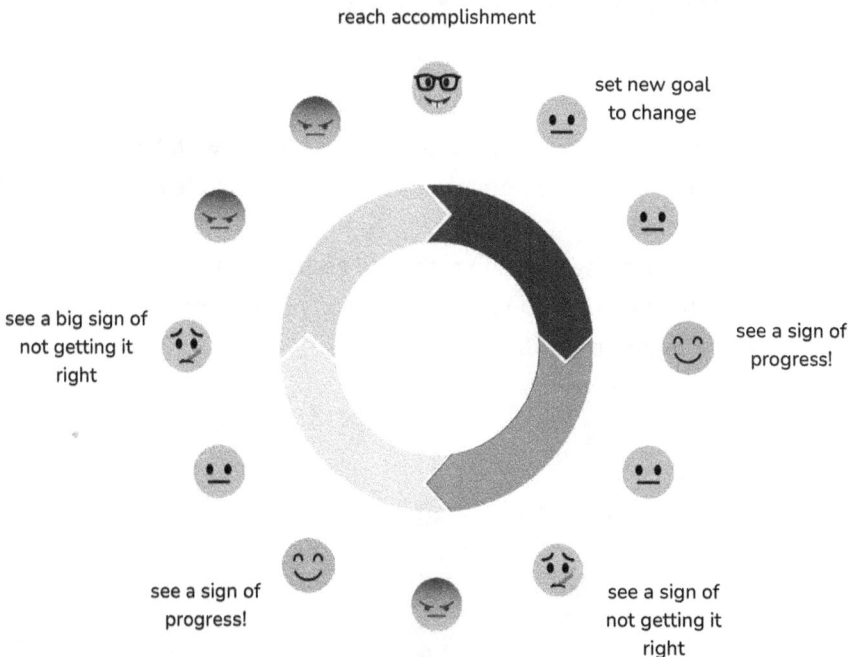

reach accomplishment

set new goal
to change

see a sign of
progress!

see a sign of
not getting it
right

see a sign of
not getting it
right

see a sign of
progress!

Anyone, at any of these seven stages, is also still divine, whole, and beautiful exactly where they are.

Latter-day Saints who only have a becoming viewpoint often appear quite eager and striving, but haggard. Their intentions are almost always pristine, but it seems like something deep inside them knows that there are never enough hours in the day to serve all the people they need to, or to become the person they're supposed to be. Their conduct is amazing, but their soul's eyes are gaunt. This is the burnout of always striving to become.

Becoming can burn you out because there's no finish line. Life feels like a roller coaster that jumps from hustle to bustle without a moment to breathe. And when your eternal salvation is at stake, slowing down doesn't feel like an option. Is this how we're supposed to be? Like gaunt saints wearing our shoes down and fingers to the bone, so we can reach an eternal finish line? When taken too far, becoming can feel like this.

AN INVITATION TO BEING

Is there no other way? In this case, there actually is. This other way is the being viewpoint. It dovetails so nicely with becoming, and allows a more generous and healthy approach to becoming, in my experience.

From the being viewpoint, there's nothing to become, no one else to be, nowhere to go. You're already here, perfect, whole, fresh, and just right. Let's dive in.

CHAPTER 2:

THE BEING VIEWPOINT

"All is well! All is well!"

This refrain from a Latter-day Saint hymn points to the fruits of the *being* perspective—no matter internal or external conditions, there is a way to be well with this moment. It's the simple joy of being.

Christ has many moments where His response to those in a stormy sea or a dark jail cell are confounding. "Be of good cheer! Take courage! Fear not!" These messages can be taken as either a very invalidating or unaware Savior, or a divine being who is seeing something from a different perspective that allows Him different responses to our disturbing conditions.

In this chapter, we'll look at what being is all about, how it might appear in church culture and doctrine, and how to begin the inside job of being whole continually.

Being   Becoming

WHAT IS BEING?

Learning to *be* is not often emphasized in church circles, in my experience, so there's a chance you may not know exactly what it looks like (without a nudge or two). It includes a deep, internal stability as the background to any moment, all things experienced as part of, and happening on, a greater plane. Resting in this wide wholeness[1] is often a soft, open, vast, knowing, and warm backdrop. This backdrop acts as the landscape to anything happening up front in our experience, like sadness, pain, fear, joy, delight, or passion.

I want to include a bit of a caveat before we move into this section. What I say in this section may feel like gobbledygook. It seemed that way to me when I started to learn about the being perspective. A lot of what I say in this section can't be proven satisfactorily with the scientific method, or in our material world, or by reading it in a book (including this one). You may have an idea of the concepts, and those concepts may land in an intellectual way, but if you're like me at all, you may not have felt it in the body—in experience.

Without direct experience, the things in this section might feel unfamiliar or confusing. They may feel like an invalidation, a bypassing of reality, or a harmful way to explain away bad things. I certainly had and sometimes still have many of these reactions. The heart of the being viewpoint is one I experience as completely confounding, and that's okay.

Please feel free to think of this section like a personally catered buffet, just for you. Walk the rows of available dishes and see if there's anything that draws you in. Take those things, and leave the rest. However, I do think there is something beautiful here, and so it may be worth leaning into each dish, giving it a good sniff, and really letting yourself get close enough to see if it's good for your system.

Unlike a traditional buffet, the dishes here will never expire. You can feel free to leave and come back as much as you like. There's really no risk to leaving it; there's probably no risk to taking it, either. You might let your gut lead you and stay open and curious with it.

---

1 I use a few phrases when talking about being, including wholeness. Philip Shepherd's book *Radical wholeness* has been instrumental in helping me wake up to an embodied sense of being.

In short, much like trying to capture God in a story or name, these descriptions cannot ever actually contain the full experience of being—they can only point to what it feels like, as well as invite you to step in for yourself. Of course, you're already, always, in being.

The **key skill of the being perspective** is to rest as our already-whole, already-free spiritual nature, and then to live from that place "at all times and in all things, and in all places that ye may be in." It is experiencing all of reality as divine light, a cycle of continual spiritual contentment.

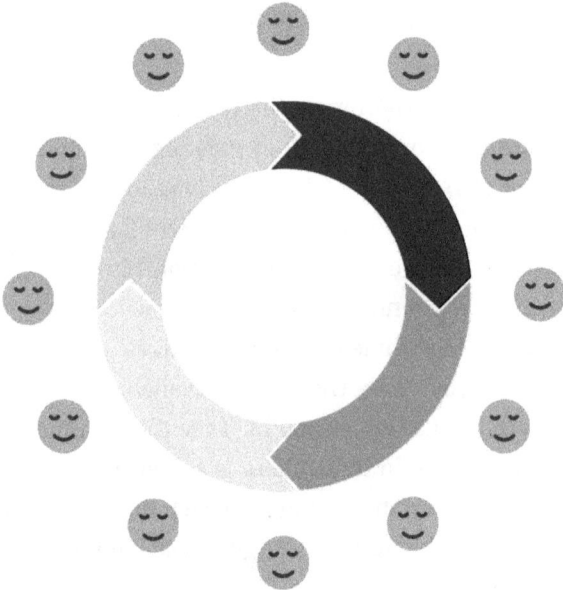

Although we are always being, and whole, perfect, and complete in that being, we fall asleep to it. Waking up to our open, natural state sometimes requires some guidance. Let's explore a few entry points that can support the falling open of the natural, whole way of being that is in each of us.

Being isn't something we do. It's not something we create, form, or accomplish. It's something that is unveiled when the conditions are right. I'll offer a few things that have been helpful for me and I'll point you to effective teachers if you really want to dive in.

First, instead of only experiencing the contents of this moment (thoughts, feelings, sensations, concepts, ideas, etc.), a being viewpoint can unveil itself when we experience the wider context or frame in which all experience is occurring. "Context creates meaning" is a common adage in the psychotherapy world. Recognizing contexts can begin to unlock being. What things mean, even tragedy and difficulty, begins to shift when being is brought into awareness.

One way the Latter-day Saint tradition invites us to open to the subtle nature of being[2] is to invite an eternal perspective, or talk about the veil of forgetfulness. To fully sit in the intensity of being mortal, with the pain, suffering, difficulty, strain, and overall momentum of living, can be overwhelming. But, when paired with the understanding that there's a bigger story here, that each of us is actually a divine Godling celebrating and evolving life in our mortal skin for a few decades, the way we relate to everyday moments can shift.

A simple way to start sensing this being perspective is to slowly zoom out on a moment. Let's try this with a practical example, like getting the flu. On its own, getting the flu can be downright miserable—aches and pains, a sore throat, snot and congestion, headaches and fever. No thank you! But, we can start to zoom out to see this hour, day, and week in context to realize that this will pass, I'm still divine, and it's all okay. From our eternal nature, this is a small moment of time that somehow also belongs as part of mortality. All is well.

Then, from our *All is well* eternal mindset, we can go back into being sick, and really be sick for the time that we're sick. Zooming out in perspective is not a way to escape from the reality of the moment, but to let some part of us stop resisting it as

2 It was helpful for me to learn about the subtle fruits of being before directly pointing to it. I attempt to offer some mental, emotional, and visual cues here that I feel can originate from being.

much, because we know we are deeply taken care of already. In the most absolute sense possible, nothing can go wrong here, whether I heal from this sickness or I don't. I am held by arms much bigger than sickness and health.[3]

Sometimes this trust builds physically, first, as happened with Joseph Smith. In the face of experimental surgery to remove an infected section of bone from his leg, it was the arms of his father that allowed him to endure the pain of the procedure, even without anesthesia. Perhaps Joseph's trust of his father's embrace on Earth prepared him to trust the embrace of a deeper spiritual field that can be seen with different eyes.[4]

When nothing can go ultimately wrong, we can drop the struggle against pain. Often, the struggle against something is more exhausting and distressing than the thing itself. Trusting an eternal okayness allows us to put our energy where we care the most—for example, in showing up for those we love—instead of putting energy into an attempt to prevent what we cannot tolerate. We can experience intensity from a place of trust and rest.

Let's play with perspective and context again, only instead of using the gospel lens of eternity, let's zoom in or out with perception. To illustrate, imagine we're going to the movies. If you tunnel in your perspective during a night at the theater, you will probably be fully and accidentally convinced for a time that you *are* the characters, the plot, and the emotion. Life (as

---

3 I think there are layers (gross, subtle, causal, and beyond) to being. In my experience so far, I've only really been able to have an absolute trust in the Divine through what I'd call being in the causal realm of experience. It has come through testing, again and again, if there's anything missing from this moment. At refined levels of being, I don't find any problems, again and again. I wonder if there are those that develop it through becoming, but I haven't felt that as much. In this book, I emphasize the fruits of being because I think both my personal life and my experience in the Church could use more of it, generally speaking.

4 My heart goes out to those who don't have arms to hold us in this life. When the physical arms in our communities don't offer their softness, how can we trust the non-physical arms? These kinds of questions bring a strong desire to hold those around me in any way possible, physically, spiritually, and emotionally, to try and emulate the holding that I believe exists beyond anything I can offer.

you know it) disappears for a while and all that exists is what's happening on the screen.

Fully immersing yourself in a movie can be deeply nourishing. Depending on what's on the screen, it can also be quite scary, intense, or damaging. Let's start zooming out and see what happens to your experience of the film's content. Maybe you look around the theater and see other people watching, you see the ceiling and walls, and smell popcorn: *Oh that's right, I'm at the local theater.* Maybe that changes how you see what's on the screen. You're still able to understand and relate to the movie, but it just has less hold on your entire condition.

You can keep watching the film while also holding, in your peripheral vision, a sense of *knowing* that what's happening is all *on a screen.* You can flip back and forth as well. Just watch the story; or, watch the story while seeing the screen too. Or, watch the story and see the walls, and smell the popcorn. Each level of zooming out will change how you experience the content on the screen. We could even change the physical setting to make it easier on you. Let's put this same movie on your phone and sit it on a bench in a busy public park at noon with the volume low. How much hold does that movie have on you now?

In the broad daylight of life, a little screen, even with highly delightsome or troubling content, doesn't have the same intensity of effect on your soul that it might otherwise. The content on the screen isn't lost to you, however. You still have full access to it. This is the power of unveiling the truth of context—we begin to pierce through unhelpful fusing with the content of a moment. The content is real, but it's not everything. From an eternal perspective, life's still good. We learn to stay in a perspective that knows that "all is well"—that this situation, at its deepest level, is still workable.

If we step briefly into modern science, we find obvious support for this message. In a psychology experiment, married women were put into an fMRI machine and shown crosses and circles flashing on a screen.[5] They were told that they would be shocked 20% of the time a cross appeared. The women reported the intensity of the shock each time one occurred. To test how the emotional and physical environment changes our *perception* and *response* to conditions (the shock), one-third of the women had their husbands hold their hand, one-third had a stranger do the same, and one-third had no one in the room with them during the experiment. As you may guess, the women who were alone showed high fMRI activity of alarm in the brain and self-reported the shock as very painful. Those with the stranger supporting them showed and reported less disturbance, and those with their husbands present had the least alarming brain activity as well as the lowest scores on experiential disturbance. What's more, the women who reported the highest marital satisfaction had the smallest threat responses. Something about knowing that they were experiencing difficulty while feeling supported and safe changed how they related to the disturbing experience. The content didn't change, but how they related to it—on a visceral, fundamental, neurological, and unconscious level—shifted.

Back to a church context: Is there anything in life that's truly unworkable? In the warm light of Christ's infinite Atonement, is there anything that can permanently go wrong? The way I see it, the war has already been won, the precious cargo is safely locked away, and we're already at our destination. That is absolutely true, always, on a spiritual level, and we can choose to join in.

I believe this is what the rest of the Lord and the Kingdom of Heaven are. The rest and the Kingdom might have a physical correlating space or time, but I also believe they are an experience that is happening now, and can always be felt, with only a few degrees shift in our awareness of a moment.

If you're a card-carrying Latter-day Saint, you may experience this phenomenon when you attend the temple. You prepare, enter, worship, serve, and then walk back out into the world. Yet, the

---

5 James Coan, Hillary Schaefer, Richard Davidson, "Lending a hand: social regulation of the neural response to threat."

world seems different. Problems seem to have less grab, struggles seem more manageable, and energy to act in impactful ways can increase. Did life actually change during your two-hour temple visit? No, of course not. The problems and challenges remain, yet the way you relate to them has shifted.

It's interesting to note, as well, that there usually isn't a moment during your temple worship where you "did the being thing." Resting in our deepest sense of being isn't actually something we achieve—that's the land of becoming. Yet, the temple revives *our realization* or *remembering* of being. In my experience, this is a complete game-changer.

The being perspective, in its fullness, unlocks an ability for humans to walk through life and feel safe, whole, and complete, regardless of the circumstance of their lives, always.

When our sense of being can stabilize, it becomes the background to any moment. Whatever pops up in the foreground (anger, sorrow, ecstasy, pain, glory, etc.), the background remains, allowing us full access to respond to foreground content instead of react to it.

Being is something you can never get out of or into. There's nowhere to actually go, nothing to do, no project to complete.

It's already here. Always. Can you feel it?

BE STILL, AND KNOW

Before moving deeper into unveiling awareness of our being, let's pause again to check in with the gospel. As I mentioned, we don't emphasize the being perspective as much in the Church. However, I'm personally noticing more and more of this stillness idea. Recently, Elder Bednar asked Latter-day Saints to "consider a higher and holier dimension of stillness in our lives—an inner spiritual stillness of the soul that enables us to know and remember" deep spiritual truth.[6] Stillness of the soul is often the very key that unlocks the being perspective. It's a kind of knowing that feels more like remembering, because we never actually leave our home of being—it's the foundation upon which all of life is happening.[7]

In my observation, we organize our church membership on a becoming spectrum, based on how much we can do:

- Active
- Less Active
- Inactive

Many people have a sense that the *active* category is most important—after all, it's how we really become like God, right? As someone decreases their activity, we might get the sense that something has gone wrong.

---

6 April 2024, General Conference, "Be Still, and Know That I Am God"

7 In church circles, we often cite that Christ is the rock upon which we should build our foundation, and it seems fitting that in contemplative Christian practices, there's sometimes not much difference between what we call God and what we call the Ground of being that we're exploring here.

Well, it's interesting that we don't organize our membership from a being perspective. We might create another spectrum, saying members are

- Super Still
- Fairly Still
- Not Still At All

It's a strange reality to me, having now sat in stillness for long periods, that this channel of the spiritual floodgates has been closed down in the Church, to some degree. Even though we aren't as open to it, I think the message is clear in the scriptures: "Be ye therefore perfect."[8] For some reason, the last time I heard this, it sounded like it was more of a present invitation rather than a future hope. If we take perfection to be a certain way we stay in our being, our awakened wholeness, Jesus is asking us to shift our perspective. None of us can actually have perfect conduct or have physical perfection. But, on the other hand, if there's a whole, perfect, and complete way of being with every moment that is, then His invitation can be fulfilled right now, and always.

Nothing can separate us from the love of God.[9] Sometimes I lose sight of this truth. In fact, for many years I think I lived as if this weren't true. I keep finding that *believing what the scriptures say* is much more difficult than listening to my small-self narratives, which are contrary to what the scriptures teach. To actually trust fall into a reality where *nothing* separates me from the love of God is much more intense and exposing than simply running my internal scripts that say *I've got to do certain things for God to love me.* (Or, maybe more accurately, *I've got to do certain things for me to love me. And when I can't love myself, how much love can I receive from anyone else?*)

When I dive deeper, I find that God's love is in and through all things. "All things" actually means "all things": the physical

---

8 Matthew 5:48

9 Romans 8:39

world of grass, trees, rocks, wind, animals; the mental world of thoughts, feelings, dreams, desires, abstractions, concepts; the spiritual world of light, formless radiance, and sacredness. Nothing can separate us from God's love because it permeates all being, all of life. Like trying to separate gravity from a tree, there's a force beyond and through it all that is constant, regardless of movement, intentions, or action.

Elder Bednar also cites, "for all flesh is in mine hands; be still and know that I am God."[10] These are absolute statements. Deepening our awareness of being allows us to physically, mentally, emotionally, and spiritually feel that we are actually held in His hands. Eventually, there are no parts of our existence that we don't experience as outside of that holding. The stillness, the truth of this reality begins to permeate the most obvious and refined parts of our inner and outer lives.

It's not lost on me that in the most sacred room of our most sacred building, there's actually nothing to do. Objectively speaking, the Celestial Room is quite a simple place. While gorgeous, pristine, and sacred, the actual physical setup is very basic—soft light, couches, and scriptures. It's interesting that in a church where many feel like they don't have permission to be still, the holiest location has nothing to do, nothing to become, no task to accomplish. Nothing to distract you from exactly *what is*.

If we can learn to sit with what is, all of life becomes sacred. We find that we're already home. In my experience, we begin to realize that there is only one home worth trusting—the sacred nature of being still and knowing a God who is the ground of all experience, a God that holds it all.

At least right now in my life, outside of being in the rest of the Lord, there is no other refuge.[11] Trust or reliance on any other source won't do the trick. When I put my relative trust in

---

10 D&C 101:16

11 "Lay not up for yourselves treasures upon earth, where moth and rust doth corrupt, and where thieves break through and steal: But lay up for yourselves treasures in heaven, where neither moth nor rust doth corrupt, and where thieves do not break through nor steal" (Matthew 6:19–20).

a sports team, bishop, partner, hobbies, spiritual teachers, or my own capacities, I end up disappointed.[12] Joseph Smith was very clear in *Lectures on Faith* that knowing the true character of God allows us to place full trust in Him. We can have absolute trust, and a trust in the Absolute. A God who falters, lies, varies, or is a respecter of persons cannot be trusted without reservation. A spiritual field of being that falters, changes, or is ever inaccessible cannot be absolute.

Having a true refuge, one that never changes nor leaves us, allows us to fully go into the fray of life. So, just be still. And watch what you can unveil.

ONE MORE LAYER

Personally, I never really found a long-term way of feeling whole while in church circles. Even when hearing personal stories about Christ's love and Atonement or hearing the heart of someone radiating gratitude, it just didn't really take, for me. That says more about my temperament, disposition, and personal experiences in the Church, perhaps, than it says about the Church at large. But, this is for those that might relate: You hear the message from the pulpit about your infinite worth and divine nature, and your stomach contracts and your chest sinks. The mind is willing, but the body is weak. I didn't develop a long-term, embodied reality of my wholeness while in an LDS chapel. That message got stuck somewhere in transit. (Again, this was probably a "me" thing, which is fine. Others might get it while at church, no problem.)

Regarding the search for greater truth and light, I'm a fan of a beautiful analogy shared by Michael Wilcox.[13] He loves drafting

---

12 2 Ne. 4:34

13 Faith Matters Podcast, "God's Many Voices"

compasses, different from the directional compasses that show true north. These drafting compasses have a pointy fixed foot that stays put while the searching foot, holding a pencil, spins around the fixed foot and draws a circle. During my burnout phase of becoming, my searching foot went out pretty far. I ended up finding the initial unfolding of this wholeness far afield from my fixed foot, via other wisdom traditions and practices.[14]

The words I shared in the last section regarding trusting in an absolute God, or mind of Christ, came only after I'd begun stabilizing in a sense of being the way other sources teach it. In addition, up until now I've used the words "being" and "wholeness" to describe the *feelings* or *state of mind* that result from a greater unveiling of the nature of being. These feelings are byproducts, not the *original thing*, per se. I've not pointed very directly at what other traditions call it: awareness, consciousness, or knowing. Often it's simply called the sacred, or source. Touching it, even once, is powerful: "There are moments of such bliss that they outshine ordinary pleasures as the sun does a firefly, moments of such love and compassion that we fall helplessly in love with all creation. A single such experience can transform your life forever."[15]

Sometimes, after someone tastes the breathless beauty of being, they aren't sure what to say about it, but they do their best to tell a story or fit it into a narrative they resonate with. The reality is, though, that our stories about it won't suffice. Calling it anything doesn't really work, as experience can show us, yet we still need ways to wake up to it. For this section, let's briefly look at how other traditions home in on being.

From Bruce Tift, a practicing Buddhist:

---

14 I know many Saints that have wholeness in church circles, and I welcome that. I also know that "anything virtuous, lovely, or of good report or praiseworthy" is part of the gospel, so it feels congruent to use Western psychology and other wisdom traditions to find the right seasonings for my palate as I attempt to find the same wholeness meal.

15 Roger Walsh, *Essential Spirituality*.

"Awareness is said to be what is most fundamental to our experiencing, a nonconceptual knowing. We will never find anything more basic, intimate, in every moment of our engagement with life."[16]

God's children in other parts of the world have discovered that this contextual zooming out process we did before can just keep going. Back to our movie theater scene—who's watching the screen and smelling the popcorn? *Why that's me!* Well, who and what are you? This question becomes the heart of the being perspective, and how we answer *who* and *what* and *where* and *when* we are changes everything.

If we really peel back the layers at any moment, we find someone, or something, experiencing every moment. In the theater example, there were layers of things happening—at first glance it was a moving picture, and then it was also a white screen upon which that picture moved. They seem like separate things that could be experienced separately, yet they also have an intimate connection.

Our minds are no different. All content appears on a screen, sometimes called *awareness* or *consciousness* or *knowing*. The content of experience is the imagery on the screen; it's always changing. The screen is awareness, the "place" where all content appears and disappears; it never changes. This is one common analogy for the mind—a screen upon which experience happens, while the screen never changes.

In fact, if we could see a time lapse of that theater *screen*, we'd see that it sits there, year after year, movie after movie, and it doesn't budge. It's always there; through the kids' shows and the horror films, the screen remains. The content on the screen doesn't actually tarnish any part of the screen, and no image can be experienced without the existence of the screen.

Again, the mind (consciousness, awareness, knowing) is the screen, the thing we rarely pay attention to, but upon which the entire film appears. The images that appear each moment are

---

16 *Already Free*, 66.

the feelings, thoughts, sensations, and perceptions that come and go in our experience.

If that analogy isn't informative, let's try using your mind and body to explore the same territory. Dropping the analogy where the screen is awareness and the movie is the contents of awareness, let's go in the opposite direction—back to you, the watcher. You can imagine you're watching a movie, or you can look at the experience of simply reading this book. You're most likely gazing at something right now, but I'll pretend you're still at the movies.

- What sees the screen? *My eyes.*
- And what experiences what your eyes see? *My brain, maybe?*
- What experiences what your brain sees? *Me.*
- Yes, you! What are you, exactly? *I'm just the thing inside that experiences what's happening.*[17]

Yes, *you are the something that is experiencing your experience.* Eventually we find a layer of "you" that we can't go beyond, a consciousness, awareness, or knowing. That is the level at which peeling back the layers often stops, because there aren't many layers past the thing that holds all the layers. Eventually an awakening can happen, and we realize that any thought, feeling, or sensation we have is happening on, as, from, and through some kind of open ground of awareness.

In general, touching into the heart of what's experiencing the moment has been important for me in experiencing the wholeness of being. There seems to be a pattern here—when someone can experience that which experiences their experience, feelings of

---

17 The Latter-day Saint may also answer, I am a spirit, or something like that. I think a close LDS correlation is intelligence, like the ones God organized in the beginning, but the gospel answer that zooms out the furthest is probably Light, the substance, source, and in-betweenness of all things. It's a spark of something—that is actually everything—that can coalesce from its infiniteness into a form and then take shape as it moves along the Plan of Salvation, ultimately always back in its original Infinite Light form, knowing itself differently forever. It's what knows, what is known, and the knowing altogether. Maybe it's also the Word from John 1:1: "In the beginning was the Word, and the Word was with God, and the Word was God." This can quickly go past the edge of my personal experience up to this point in my life, so I won't say much more here.

softness, openness, love, acceptance, presence, patience, charity, and hope begin to arise spontaneously. (These also seem to correlate with the fruits of the Spirit.) From the ground of open awareness, any content that pops up on the screen of awareness is interpreted and experienced differently. We become more available to respond with wisdom, rather than react out of habit or emotion. Agency feels very different. This is how being begins to help us become what we truly intend, as we'll soon explore.

This kind of recognition of awareness is not a common topic in Latter-day Saint circles. As such, there's a good chance that you haven't been an observer of your experiences, or been shown how to get there. Or, you may have unveiled it on your own. While noticing your experience in this way isn't required for a beautiful life, it's also fully available to anyone who seeks, or stumbles into it. Again, you can't actually get "into" or "out of" being, so these metaphors really speak more to the waking up to the wholeness of being, not the production or transformation of it. The reality is that you are the self you know now, and you are this open awareness, just waiting to wake up to itself.

Being never changes. It never grows or shrinks. It never transforms or becomes anything. Whatever you were before you had a body, or a spirit, or were organized as an intelligence, that thing that just keeps experiencing, that's being. It always just is. It's the ground of all existence, the formless womb that births every moment.

A short reference for **being**	
Basic Essence	Being with what is. A non-judgmental, non-interpretive field. A sensibility beyond the distinctions between good/bad, self/other, now/later—it's always *just this*. Maintains an innate, unconditional kindness and "Yes" to what's here now. Immediacy—closing the distance *between our experience* and *the field in which, and of which, it is.*
Deals With	Changing how we relate to content/circumstances.

Fruits of balance	Peace, acceptance, the rest of the Lord, open-ness—"be still, and know that I am God." Feeling whole, continually.
Fruits when taken too far	Numbness, apathy, indifference, disconnection, fear of losing identity; we appear checked out, aloof, in the clouds, un-impacted.
Tendencies when in balance	Ability to be with things as they are, deep presence and availability with everything and everyone. Attitude of unconditional kindness to self, other, and world.
Tendencies when taken too far	Can lead to inaction, neglect, sins of omission. Disregarding the immediate, relative realities of life.

THE INTERIOR SENSIBILITY OF BEING WHOLE

This quality of being is largely an inside job, meaning it happens on the very subjective level of our interior experience. Someone who lives from this place can find a deep rest in their physical body, an abiding calm in their emotional life, and a profound serenity in their awareness.[18]

The interior sensibility of being begins to open the possibility that every moment is workable, and that the quality of our wellbeing isn't determined by internal or external circumstance. Internal circumstances could be fear, depression, hearing the inner critic, etc.; external circumstances are the weather, how clean our houses are, a partner's behavior, the cancellation of an airline flight, etc. Eventually the distinction between inside and outside dissolves and everything has a similar, delicious, sacred taste to it. It's a liberating experience. In contrast to feeling like I have armor on, to protect against the world, it feels more like a spacious field, an open canvas, or a continual hug of each moment.

---

18 John Kesler, *Integral Polarity Practice in Service of Leadership for Flourishing.*

To bring in some imagery, as we rest in a cozy winter cabin, storms may rage and winds may blow, but our wellbeing stays intact. This is experiencing intensity from a place of stability. And, when we carry this inner stability into every moment, even when the winter storm blows in through the front door, the power goes off, and the family is squabbling, our innermost chambers still smile kindly on each happening, knowing how to stay whole amidst comings and goings of life.

The work of *finding* our innate goodness and being, as you can see in previous sections, can seem like tough work that requires a deep trust. To truly open to each moment and sense it in its perfection requires us to go beyond our old familiar narratives, give up struggling against embodied discomfort, and be radically present. At its heart, however, the "work" of being is really just falling open. It's doing less. As one mentor shared, "Just soften up and be here."[19]

This "work" is yours to do, even as you're already being it.

Although this sounds simple enough, fully unfurling into it is sometimes much slower or more elusive than we like. I frequently invite clients to tap into their innate wholeness. After they've cognitively understood that, *yes, they are always divine on some level,* they try to feel it in their heart and body. But it doesn't take. They can know the concept in their mind, yet their physiology and emotions don't come along for the ride.

This is such a real struggle. Perhaps some additional metaphors and music can help set the mood for wholeness to be settled into. Let's massage your mind, heart, and body, each in turn:

---

19 Geoff Fitch, with Pacific Integral.

Rational Mind

At what age are kids the best? The most perfect? Ironically, if we could do a language survey by eavesdropping on parents, we'd probably find that babies are the most perfect. It's strange. Objectively, babies are the worst humans—they take all your time, stretch your budget, literally suck the life out of you (for nursing mothers), ruin your sleep, and give you that constant poop smell on your hands no matter how many times you wash them. Honestly, babies can be the worst humans!

But they are so perfect! *Perfect* is such a common word I hear around babies. "Aren't you just perfect! Look at you, your little toes, your nose—oh my gosh, he's opening his eyes!" When was the last time you were celebrated for *opening your eyes*?? I mean, come on, most of us can't get praise for anything these days. Babies get it for nothing.

And, we kiss their fat rolls. Seriously, if you were lucky enough to have parents that loved you, they most likely literally kissed the fat of your thighs, neck, and face. When was the last time someone kissed all the parts of you that jiggle? Babies can't even ask for it and they get it all the time; many of us could beg for it and not get an ounce of it.

Is this making sense? Can your mind grasp this insane reality? That the most "useless" humans are getting all of the love, admiration, and unconditional affection? This isn't by mistake, I don't think. Something in us knows there's a perfection there. We originate from a perfect essence, without doing or becoming anything. Then, somewhere along the way, we get the sense that we can and should become something better. We want to become something. And just like that, our perfection seems to vanish.

Or does it? Did perfection leave us, or did we leave the recognition of perfection?

I'm pretty sure you're better (more skilled and useful) than an infant right now—why doesn't anyone treat you better than an infant? Do you treat yourself better than you treat infants? It would be very illogical not to do so, because you're clearly more useful (e.g. you can read!) than infants. Of course, usefulness doesn't equate to your value, but come on—on that rational mind level, it's a no brainer.

It's my belief that there's still something in you that hasn't budged an inch since you were an infant, and even before. It's your innate being-ness. It's what has experienced all of your experiences, and will continue experiencing them all, and it is perfectly the same as it always has been. Bright. Lucid. Vast. One.

As a rational mind practice, ponder and write down five ways you can treat a loved one with the perfection you perceive in an infant. Also write down five ways in which you could treat yourself as if you were still perfect in some way. Make a plan to carry these out.

Heart

Have you ever hugged someone, but they didn't let your hug go through? Usually it's for good reasons, but to the one doing the hugging, it just feels like tension and bracing. For this section, just notice the being nature of your heart.

Imagine a loved one entering the space you're in. You don't need to see them, but you can if you like. Don't just see them in your mind, feel them from an open heart. Feel their unique signature on this moment. Feel their warmth begin to wash through the space.

Imagine they approach you with open arms and heart. Anything that usually holds them back is gone; they can be here with you, perfectly. Open your heart. Don't let their hug get stuck between you. Opening your heart doesn't actually require action. In fact, sometimes it just falls open when you *stop doing tension*.

Open Heart might be your default state. Let yourself return to openness by not having to do a thing. Like the act of bringing in the groceries, you set the bags down by *releasing* your grip, not by *doing some extra action*. You simply *cease to do holding*. Allow yourself that easing. Cease holding back.

As Open Heart, the being channel is here; your beloved can minister to you with love, radiance, words, laughter, touch, memory, and the unspoken beauty of communion.

Just be here now. Let yourself be impacted.

Body

Another gateway to being is to awaken to the reality that your body is continually moving with perfection and completeness from moment to moment. Even as you read, notice how you breathe. Most likely, you haven't had to manage your breath at all. Yet, you get it perfectly right.

Your digestion, your hormones, your cell regrowth, your heart beating, your temperature regulation. You are basically doing a trust fall right now, in this moment, into your body, and without any trying at all, you get it right.

Certainly, disease strikes, things get imbalanced, and bodies decline. And sometimes that can be the right "next thing," like an oak tree taking its life horizontal, to find its next stage of decay and regrowth.

However, in general, most of us have had thousands and thousands of hours of getting our physical beingness completely right, all without effort. What a miracle. It can be helpful a few times a day to take your pulse, feel your breath, and remember on a deep level that life is trying to keep you going.

Just sit and feel how right your body is, with or without any of your conscious attention. Mortal bodies have a way of being that just wants to keep on being, for the most part.

Give up any struggle against gravity. We subconsciously clench our muscles, as if gravity is going to fail us at any moment. Give up the fight. No more struggle.

Sense through your body the micro-bracing that some of your muscles are doing, and just let gravity have its way with you. Fall into her arms.

Let your body just do its thing, let it love to be as it is. Surrender into physical trust, complete trust, that this moment holds you.

The ground isn't going anywhere. Trust it.

DEEPER GROUND

As a student of these teachings, it's important for me to note that I'm just scratching the surface here. There are even more grand, more fundamental, and more empty and full areas of practice that I don't speak about here. See the footnotes for more resources.[20]

LIMITATIONS OF THE BEING PERSPECTIVE

The being perspective has gems that cannot be mined elsewhere. There are also key pitfalls here when being is taken too far, including a sense of indifference, bypassing real difficulty or suffering, and an inability to act.

Someone who goes too far into the being perspective will sometimes assume that because they can find peace in disturbance, it means others can as well, so nothing needs to change. This goes too far and misses the mark—suffering is real, pain is real, and abuse is real. Just because someone can internally accept the fullness of the moment doesn't mean everyone can, nor does it

---

20 This is where a teacher or mentor can come in handy. I have several teachers that I reference throughout the book. For the Latter-day Saint who wants to stay close to the tradition while exploring this territory, I don't know of anyone better than John Kesler and Thomas McConkie. There are others in these realms that are doing great work, but these are just the ones I've been drawn to working with. They also have many students and colleagues to refer you to that offer incredible coaching, therapy, and training in addition to, and in support of, what John and Thomas bring.

If anything I'm sharing in the being section is piquing your interest, I hope my words make you hungrier and more confused, as opposed to satisfied and clear about what's going on with awareness. Honestly, what these teachers can share has incredible richness, depth, and fullness, and I can't recommend working with them enough. Integral Polarity Practice (John's powerful framework to support living a sacred life—LDS and otherwise) is perhaps the most impactful practice I've done to benefit my growth in this area. What John and Thomas bring to this territory, which is quite absent in the Church, is a new horizon to the faith that feels like it's arriving just in time to meet what life is demanding of each of us. For many people, tapping into these rich wellwaters of being can only happen when facilitated by a master of the territory. Anything short of working with a true master teacher is a pale replacement for the genuine experience, as far as I can tell.

mean that nothing is to be done. A more complete experience of being will naturally lead to appropriate action for the benefit of all.

A term used in this context is *spiritual bypassing*, which means that by taking a "bigger" spiritual perspective (eternal perspective), people think problems disappear. It's often a great way to actually avoid intensity, disturbance, and the get-your-hands-dirty work. Transcending a moment via spiritual practice so you don't have to engage the moment distorts reality and kills compassionate service.[21]

I had a very vivid lesson of this during one of my first big peak experiences of pure being as awareness. The world shifted dramatically for me and all of life just seemed to be unfolding before my eyes in its radiance and light, lasting for three days and nights. Everything seemed to have the same taste and I found myself smiling contentedly no matter what was happening.

At one point during this experience, we were having a family pizza night and our kids were running around the kitchen and living room—one with a pizza cutter and the others with glasses of water spilling everywhere. My wife was understandably frazzled from the chaos, and even more frazzled with my response to the moment: I just calmly smiled and laughed at the beauty of the moment.

I felt as if it was perfect. Nothing needed to change! I lazily meandered around the kitchen to get some food with them. After putting them to bed a few hours later, I was still feeling good vibes (no substances involved, by the way), and she told me that she didn't feel like I was "here" any longer. *What do you mean*, I thought, *I'm standing right here talking to you.* She told me she felt that I couldn't see her distress or take her experience into account, and even that my visual gaze was looking *past* her.

This is an extreme example from my life, but it proved an important point for me: Spiritually escaping into the acceptance of anything and everything is incomplete when it detaches from the lived reality of life. I wasn't reactive, but I also wasn't responsive.

---

21 See chapter on Eternal Partnership for more about the "God Block" in couples.

I was just *being there*. What of my children's physical safety? What of my wife's heart? When being claims that All is Well and cannot act with compassion, it can become a limitation.

INTERLUDE: A STORY FOR THE SOUL

Sometimes stories can massage a message deeper into our bones, beyond what a chart or explanation ever could. Here's a story to cleanse the palette before the next course.

THE UNTOUCHABLE ROYAL

Once upon a time, a king and queen ruled graciously over their land, blessing each member of their community. They looked forward to having children, and within a few years, a princess and a prince were born. The twins were beloved by all, especially by their parents.

Of course, the custom of the time was to bring up the children to one day govern and rule in place of the king and queen. In fact, no other person had the right to—only royals could rule. As the twins matured into teenagehood, they asked their parents how this all worked.

"So we're supposed to rule the kingdom one day?" the twins asked.

"Why yes, it's your birthright! You are royal," responded the parents.

"But when did we get our royalness?"

"You've always had it."

"Always? Even before we were born?"

"Well, yes, actually, in a way. We've always had it, you've always had it, your kids will always have it... It's just the nature of things in our lineage."

"I don't remember getting it. Are you *sure* we have it?" the teens asked.

"We are. As surely as you breathe, it is you," the parents beamed.

The twins didn't really get it. *A thing that they never remember getting, that they have never seen, that they never really know as different or special in their experience?* Sounds trippy, and they certainly thought so. It was the water they swam in.

As teens often do, they got tired of filling the expectations of others. They found themselves slinking into town more often, looking for adventure. The delights of life seemed exotic and enticing to them, and one night they did not return to the castle.

The king and queen went out with search parties and eventually found them in the early hours of the morning in a drunken stupor outside of a party hall. They had enjoyed every pleasure the city had to offer, against the advice of their parents.

After their parents loved them, cleaned them, and brought them back into the castle walls, the twins finally came to their senses. They felt awkward and a bit embarrassed, regretting some (but not all) of their evening adventures. They did not feel very royal.

"We're so sorry. Please don't kick us out!" the twins begged.

"Of course we won't, we love you. There is space for all of you, no matter what that looks like," the parents reassured.

"Well, I guess that blows our *royal family lineage...*" they said, eyes down.

"Nope."

"What do you mean? We did exactly what you told us not to. You said the delights of the city wouldn't satisfy us and it wasn't the *royal way.*"

"That's right. But your royalty can't be affected by you. It's outside of your reach. You don't hold your royalty; it holds you. Nothing you do or don't do can impact the fact of your royalness."

For several months after that, the twins had renewed vigor for their royal duties. They learned foreign languages, practiced their music, debated their teachers, learned etiquette and beauty customs, served the poor, and tirelessly tried to become the role they were born for.

Once after an especially long day and near-perfect performance at all their tasks, the twins sat at dinner feeling very self-satisfied.

"Well, Mom and Dad, it looks like we might be royal after all!" they beamed.

"What do you mean, children? Of course you are," the queen and king replied.

"I mean look at us—we're actually living into our royalty! We're *really* royalty now."

"On the contrary, our dear Princess and Prince—you're no more royal than you were last year."

"But come on, can't you say we seem more royal right now? I mean check us out—the spitting image of a true princess and prince!" the twins grinned, awaiting the approval of their parents.

"We do love you, that is true. But again, your royalty can't be affected by you. It's outside of your reach. You don't hold your royalty; it holds you. Nothing you do or don't do can impact the fact of your royalness."

The words of their parents echoed through their heads all evening, filling their dreams, and unraveling their assumptions. *How can something be outside of our impact, yet be such a part of us? What do we do about such a thing? How do we get it right? Or wrong?*

One day amidst their routines, seemingly for no reason at all, a wave of softness came over them. They felt their brows unfurrow, their breath settle down into their core, and the world fell out beneath them. Trust. Knowing. *We are royal.*

This became a mantra they often repeated to each other. Every time they said it, something felt more real, available, and generous inside them. Something beyond them moved through their words, actions, and intentions. It was always there, no matter what they did or didn't do. It was born from nothing and yet seemed to keep coming to life. They couldn't make it bigger or smaller, couldn't make it change in any way. It was perfect no matter what, no matter what they were. And they believed it.

It was a palace of nowhere, but they took it everywhere they went. They began living, serving, and loving in a new way. Without a thing to get right or wrong, the pressure left. No one was keeping score and there was always enough—it never seemed to run out. *What does royalty do now, or say now, or love now?* The world was wide open.

With nowhere to go, nowhere to hide, nowhere to escape to, royalty had them in its fullness. They beamed with a light rarely found in rulers, and they brought an immense generosity of love to every moment of their service, infusing their lands and their people with a life beyond the wildest of fairy tales.

The End.

PART II: THE WORK

When these perspectives join together with the same mission, magical things happen.

CHAPTER 3:

JOINING BECOMING AND BEING VIEWS

Perhaps you can taste how becoming and being are each essential in our human journey. So, what happens when the two collide? Is it possible that they take turns? Or do they inform each other? Perhaps they can even show up at the same time.

In this section, we'll explore what it's like after each side has been filled out, as well as how life changes forever after this happens. We'll open a field for both to bump into each other, dance with each other, or co-create each other. Perhaps the Church is a place where we can see both in their deepest light and shadow.

Let's Check In:

We've spent a few chapters talking separately about becoming and being as distinct human dispositions, with their unique gifts and limitations, and now we'll see what it's like when they begin interacting. For many of us, we can initially only live from one quality at a time—some are accustomed more to being, others to becoming. Much like a sports team always playing the same starting line-up, we can get accustomed to relying on certain players while benching others.

As we progress, we become adept at knowing when to lean on one quality or the other in a dynamic process. This initial skill is a move from a "one or the other" mindset to something like "either one can be a great way to go, depending on the situation." We begin to reduce the rigidity or exclusive reliance on one side and taste greater freedom and agility in life.

Being   Becoming

BOTH ARE TRUE

Well-intentioned church members can get stuck here. Should I lean into "be still, and know that I am God" or into "go and do the things which the Lord hath commanded me" today? We ask: *God, which commandment should I break?* It's a relatable dilemma, and one that may never get resolved. It's my hope to invite a shift from an either/or position to a both/and position.

Depending on where you're at with each of these perspectives, you may feel a stronger urge toward either becoming or being. This is normal. Most of us have a preference toward one, initially. As we invite the less familiar side to speak up, and as we attempt to embody and explore it, it can seem a bit weird, or it can be completely liberating. Just notice your experience of each side so far.

You may have a magnetic pull to deepen into one side for a while, even months or years at a time. That can be healthy, but of course can be overdone. For many of us, at some point, we can begin to see that going too far into either side is limiting in some way.

If we are stuck in becoming, our ability to fully embrace this moment, in all of its liveliness, is often hampered in favor of a future moment. We don't fully participate in the *now* because we are so set on what could be, and the moving target of what could be builds a habit in us of looking to *what is not*, instead of *what is*.

Getting stuck in being, without recognizing the essential nature of transformation, can get us lost in the clouds of All is Well. We can cultivate beautiful states of oneness and acceptance, fully accepting this moment, but not know how to translate these inner spaces into daily tasks, meaningful systemic impact, or holistic relationships.

Luckily, there's no rule that only one viewpoint is right. Both have their truth, their place, their light and shadow.

When we deepen into each side independently, we find both treasures and pitfalls. We want the transformation and we also want the satisfaction with the now. We want Christ's Atonement to purify and heal us—truly transform us—and we want to know that God is holding us always, even right now. Because my experience in the Church has led me to feel a deep lack on the being side, I've intentionally been overcompensating, both in my life and in this text. My hope is to invite you to really saturate here and see if there is fruit or not.

A delightful psychotherapist[1] recommends a two-step process here, which I think of like a two-step authentication when you want to log in to a digital account. It's helpful for me, because it reminds me that to really unlock the fullness of this moment, both parts are essential:

1) Fully embrace and accept the moment in all of its truth (being).
2) From this place of acceptance, genuinely wonder how to improve the situation (becoming).

The first step allows us to give up all struggle, release tension, and be open to the moment. The being approach is essential to embody fully the reality that this moment is whole, as are we, on a very deep level, regardless of the details of life. From this field of resounding spiritual abundance, we can now look with new eyes at how to move forward and make this moment its best possible version. (*Best possible* is usually related to things like less suffering, more equity, more compassion, etc. Fruits of the Spirit.)

A short reference for **Both/And (being & becoming join)**	
Basic Essence	"Each of you is perfect the way you are... and you can use a little improvement."[2]
	Can accept what is, feeling whole, while becoming.
	"being there, while getting there."[3]

1 Bruce Tift, *Already Free.*

2 Shunryu Suzuki

3 Lama Surya Das, Edge of Mind podcast interview with Andrew Holecek.

Deals With	Both relating to and changing content/ circumstances.
Fruits of balance	Feelings of acceptance, trust, and openness, while feeling progress, transformation, and innovation as we engage full-heartedly in life.
Fruits of over/underuse	Only emphasizes one side; can idolize a both/and perspective, creating another thing to achieve or be; demands to feel whole in both foreground *and* background; feelings of zealousness and exclusivism.
Tendencies when in balance	Moves through life very presently, with unconditional kindness to self, other, and world, often manifesting as intelligent, potent action and service.
Tendencies when over/underused	Only emphasizes one side; can get too attached to personal or spiritual growth; can feel distant, pushy, or prideful to others.

There is a deep wisdom here that is hard to speak, but easy to feel. If I walk into my kitchen and it's a mess, I can feel a sense of frustration, failure, or judgment. If I move into cleaning from *those* feelings, cleaning happens in a very particular manner—usually with lots of silence, tension, and huffing.

On the other hand, if I can witness the mess, pause to fully accept all of the ensuing sensations, thoughts, and feelings, and realize they are as much a part of this moment as my innate goodness, I already feel whole. I don't clean the kitchen to *become* whole or even to *feel better*. Instead, I clean because I delight in a tidy space for me and my family.

I can move through life pursuing what I value, find beautiful, and hold sacred, instead of moving through life based on what I *must have happen in order to feel better inside.*

Does that make sense? Often we clean the kitchen so we can finally 1) put our mind at ease, 2) feel accomplished, or 3) do our duty, because we're not sure how to 1) ease our mind, 2) feel innately accomplished, or 3) disidentify from our "duty." So we move into kitchen cleaning as the solution to an internal problem we don't have any other way of fixing. Life becomes a series of actions organized around keeping us out of our disturbing feelings, sensations, and beliefs.

If this continues, roads in life begin to close. Like I mentioned previously regarding agency, true agency means that both poles are open: I can clean or not clean the kitchen. But most of us feel disturbingly compelled to do one or the other in order to feel complete inside.

When we start from our innately whole being, our contracted internal feelings aren't the guiding criteria for our actions. We can use more virtuous foundations for our engagement, like what we value, what the Spirit is prompting, or what seems most good, true, and beautiful.

Outside of all of the nice "wholeness and innate goodness" stuff, it's also just more economical to operate from acceptance and wholeness. People may resist the idea of radical acceptance, saying, 'So if my house is on fire, I should just accept it?' Of course not! You have to improve the situation so you don't die. But, let's ask: *From what internal place should I complete these tasks?* My personal experience has been that even in moments of danger, intensity, or crisis, starting from an internal place of acceptance is a more effective path to success.

Those who start any task with a mind like a placid lake will have access to more of themselves, and they'll think more clearly. Start whole, perfect, complete, and your chances of ending up so actually increase.

All of this is much more easily said than done. How on earth can we hold a state of being while becoming is so important?

We've got to "get bigger."4

---

4 I first heard it this way from Thomas McConkie. I've heard Ken Wilber say, "transcend and include" as well, and John Kesler uses that phrase in his Integral Polarity Practice, which I highly recommend for this territory.

GETTING BIGGER

There's a sensibility in the mind, body, and heart that allows being and becoming to be experienced at the same time.

As a little practice, imagine just zooming out a bit with your gaze right now. If you're reading this book, just soften your gaze as you read. Realize that in a softness of vision you can read these words fully while also sensing the world around you. You can see what's behind this book, while also fully reading each word. If you clench down too hard with your vision, you'll lose it. Feel into it gently, just softly allowing the essence of the words as well as the background and periphery.

You can also expand this to sound. Read these words while calmly taking stock of sounds around you. And again, you might contract or shrink, and lose this expanded sensing. But staying big and vast, sounds don't distract from reading, they just hold reading as it happens right in front of you. This is reading, in the context of hearing.

Lastly, sensations can be felt while reading. Notice how simply seeing the word *posture* brings your own posture sensations into experience, maybe even inviting some changes. You're bigger than these words, than this book. Yet you are fully with it, and with everything around you as well.

You can now get bigger than being and becoming. It might feel like holding one in each hand. You can see them both in their own uniqueness. Being is vast, serene, without resistance, and unchanging. Becoming seeks, desires, and knows something not yet created. Maybe you can even feel the space between them. What do you notice about each from this wider vantage point that you didn't before?

Some people feel a strong repulsion between the two, while others feel a sense of union or collaboration. Notice what this is like for you. Keep softening as you go and trace the edge between them. When does becoming stop and being begin? If I'm becoming something new and better, don't I only do that in the now? Can I be anywhere else except for right here, right now? I'm always a human being.

And when I'm grounded in being fully in a moment, doesn't that moment lead to a kind of transformation, intentional or not? Can we actually ever not be in being or becoming? It seems, at some level, like they permeate each other in each moment.

From a bigger perspective, we learn to transcend and include each of these views. We go beyond them, while holding their fullness.[5]

For me, this is the best of both worlds. It isn't a compromise between the two, or even a fifty-fifty split. It's both gifts, in their fullness, held together in a both/and spiritual field. This is the place from which I can be whole always while I'm becoming the best version of me. From here, there's no such thing as an underdeveloped moment.[6]

In the life cycle of an oak tree, when is it perfect? When is it "done?" Is the tree ever not perfect? Is it ever not becoming? From a seed, to sprout, to sapling, to mature tree, to dead and fallen, to rot and decay, to nourishing the next seed, is it ever not perfect? Each part feels complete, yet different and dynamic.

In the language of being and becoming, the tree is always completely whole as it is. Yet, certain ways of transforming are more fitting for the context. Do you need flour for pancakes? Acorn is probably best. Do you need shade? Take the adult tree in summer. Do you need to find spiders and centipedes? Find a decaying log.

---

5 Again, I can't emphasize enough how useful experiential work in this territory is. Specifically, I've been really impacted by Connirae Andreas' Wholeness Process, John Kesler's Integral Polarity Practice (including Thomas McConkie's retreats), the faculty and offerings at Pacific Integral, and Dustin DiPerna's Rigdzin sangha and Mahamudra retreats.

6 Chögyam Trungpa Rinpoche

> When we're bigger, we see *Tree* in its glory and beauty today, as well as its transformational trajectory. We don't have any need to disparage the seedling or sapling. *Tree* becomes not a fixed object, but a process. We can delight in every stage of Treedom, yet still know which aspects of Tree are more suitable to the moment. Seeing Tree for only what it is right now, or only as it can become, leaves its beauty unearthed.

Regarding our own being and becoming, they can dance together, supporting each other to be what's needed for the moment. Based on my own imbalances, I advocate for resting as whole while engaging in becoming. But, honestly, wherever we're at is totally fine as well. (And, it can improve.)

FOREGROUND AND BACKGROUND

One way to approach this both/and, or transcend and include, perspective is the metaphor of foreground and background. I was once at a training for couples therapists and the trainer played a video of someone walking by a lake on a forest trail. The first time, there was no music. The second time he played it, there was scary music. The third time he played it, there was delightful music.

Context creates meaning, so, of course, the experience of each round of the video was so different for me. Thoughts, feelings in the body, reactions—all of these shifted automatically with the background music.

Taking this into a church context, I sometimes experience lessons or teachings with unhelpful background music playing. Imagine a stern-looking man pointing his finger at you, "Go and sin no more!" Phew! That can be a gut punch.

Now, imagine the kindest eyes and warmest heart you can, inviting, "Go, and sin no more!" You're free, you're liberated, you're whole, even now. And always.

Let's Check In:

After we find ourselves choosing either being or becoming without too much difficulty, a beautiful possibility begins to emerge: What if the gifts of both are simultaneously available to me?

This shift is most transformational, in my experience, when being stabilizes as a backdrop to all of the happenings of becoming. We can rest in a deep sense of acceptance, embrace, and kindness to all that is occurring in the moment, and then meet the relative changes that need to happen with greater capacity.

Most importantly for me is the felt experience that a part of me never increases or diminishes, regardless of the ups and downs of mortal life. An innate goodness, beyond my ability to impact it, always shepherds the moment.

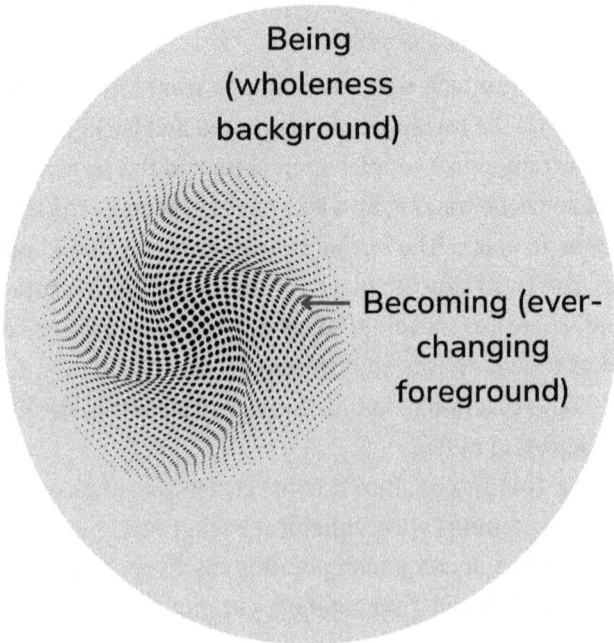

Being (wholeness background)

Becoming (ever-changing foreground)

For me, resting deeply in wholeness is an essential first step to becoming what God calls me to become. Wholeness, and its fruitful feeling of the rest of the Lord, has become a background upon which anything in the foreground is workable, as long as I can maintain it. Wholeness is a sense of abundance, of Yes, of All is Well, that instead of distancing or disengaging me from the moment does just the opposite. Knowing the sun is always shining allows a deeper dive into the storm, for no storm is bigger than the sun. Knowing my bungee cord is triple secured allows me the freedom to dive off the bridge more confidently. All of these are the liberating paradox of experiencing disturbance from a place of okayness.

As a last metaphor, wholeness is what it's like to be Ocean. Waves on an endless sea can rise and fall. A big wave can even overwhelm a smaller wave. But no wave can overwhelm the ocean. As Ocean, all Waves are you. And you are bigger than Waves. If you get stuck thinking you are Wave, you can be overwhelmed, broken to pieces, and annihilated. But no wave can pester the Ocean. Be Ocean. Be whole. And anything that arises on your surface you will know and greet as it is—a part of you, and you, but not all of you. Be Ocean.[7]

"The wind and waves obey my will; peace, be still."[8]

BOTH AT CHURCH

What's it like to attend church from wholeness?
What's it like to repent from wholeness?
What's it like to take the sacrament from wholeness?
What's it like to set yearly ward mission goals from wholeness?

7 if you don't become the ocean
you'll be seasick every day
-Leonard Cohen, "Good Advice For Someone Like Me"

8 Hymn 105, "Master, the Tempest is Raging"

Strangely enough, some perspectives on the gospel give evidence that these wholeness/being approaches aren't possible, and maybe aren't even healthy. From one angle, the Church is giving us our problem (we're fallen, estranged from God) and conveniently providing the solution (Atonement via ordinances by correct authority, among other things). So, to start whole doesn't really seem to fit the plan. Doesn't the plan require us to be broken, wounded, and fallen?

How can Jesus be our advocate with the Father if we're already whole? Do we just tell Jesus that "we've got this already handled!" and He can step aside?

The answers are yours to find.

But, as a fellow traveler, here are some personal thoughts on the matter. There's also an entire section near the end of the book where Saints like you and me share their experience of this living paradox. And, spoiler alert, the answers aren't always tidy, much like Jesus's responses to life's biggest questions.

To get us started, if we lean too hard into becoming, the gospel becomes a spreadsheet that rates our worthiness every second of every day. The worthiness ticker may have the tendency to flicker up and down all day every day, and we can become more and more neurotic about each thought, action, feeling, and desire. Scrupulosity can enter the scene and smother all the goodness that we are. God becomes a strict judge that is nearly impossible to appease; we're never good enough. We never rest. Our soul becomes gaunt. We live from a stance of eternal bracing.

This doesn't feel like the good news to me.

The being side answers the above question by saying that nothing in our immediate experience is actually beyond the capacities of the Atonement. We are held, even now, regardless of circumstance, by a field of spiritual light that never fades. We are whole, and can always stay that way because we are inseparable from God's love. Everything is groovy and chill, baby. Just trust, and relax. All is well.

This *feels* better to some people, but incomplete. Aren't we supposed to do stuff too? People are in real pain, right now.

When being and becoming join hands, however, something beautiful happens. We find that we are, indeed, moving from fullness to fullness, resting in God's love and perfection and power, always. From this place, we join Christ in accomplishing incredible and indispensable feats of healing, love, and transformation. We can depend deeply on Christ and others, and trust ourselves. We join up with Christ as partners, true partners, honoring the divine light that is already flowing through us and Him and all around us. Saviors on Mount Zion.

Our fallen nature and wounding become features along the path of ever-present wholeness, to be brought fully onto the path with love and embrace. No stagnation or orphaning of our experience is required, and our transformation begins to unfold from a radiating source of goodness that is just taking its time as it encompasses more and more of our nature. Like food dye dumped into a pool, a natural, gradual saturation of all particles takes place, wholeness permeating every moment as the pool reveals itself in unified, unique, ever-changing divine color.

Attending church from wholeness can mean that we don't need anything to happen from church, but we attend out of our love and abundance for life. It may also mean that we need the Church deeply, relying, depending, and submitting to the supportive arms of the ward members. Our innate wholeness can sense needs arising that can be nourished by community, sacrament, and fasting, and so from a deep trust, we allow ourselves to manifest our brokenness or woundedness even more deeply.

Brokenness, from a place of despair and hopelessness, has to monitor itself, else it actually lead to the abyss of supposed annihilation. But brokenness, from a place of wholeness, can go deeper than deep without any fear of permanent damage. Ironically, the trust allows the plunge that seems to abandon all trust.

We can risk it all when we're backgrounded in wholeness. Repentance can be complete, a full return to what we already are, without shameful residue. Freshness is every moment as our conduct gradually becomes more and more refined for the sacredness of each moment.

WIDENING CIRCLES

It's my understanding that our maps of how the gospel is to be lived are intimately connected to our perspectives. When I come from a scarcity and "never enough" mindset, the gospel can only be a salve for my lack. When I come from a place of fullness and abundance, the gospel is a beautiful addition to what's already gestating. In fact, there's less and less distinction between what I call myself and what I call God.

I believe that as our membership rests as wholeness more consistently, how we talk and teach about basic gospel principles will change. The heart of the doctrines won't shift, as I see it, but how we bring those principles into our hearts, souls, and service will evolve. They'll take on new dimensions that we couldn't see before, yet that were here all along.

Missionary service might become a collaborative, inter-faith celebration of God's ever-present light, no matter the denomination or dispensation. Sharing the gospel might sound more like sharing our open, eternal eyes with others, witnessing them in their fullness.[9] Confessing and repenting could become a blissful tune-up regarding our unification with the Divine. Gospel ordinances could shift from a mandatory safety net to a symbolic expression of what's already here, emerging.

Our external actions may begin to find more fertile ground in our inner experience. Wanting to create a physical Zion may turn our hearts back on themselves, creating an internal oneness with all parts of us. Redeeming the dead of the past may also include

---

9 A Faith Matters interview with Thomas McConkie inspired these thoughts.

returning to claim our internal orphans, re-immersing ourselves in proxy for our younger past selves in order to liberate our present. If we currently get stuck washing and anointing our bodies in memorized repetition, we may instead continually feel the Spirit also washing our minds and hearts, memorizing the feeling of moment-to-moment falling away of the scales from our eyes.

As our circles widen with greater perspective, it seems that being and becoming will birth a new spiritual and physical gospel landscape that none of us could architect before it emerges. I can almost feel it co-arising, even now.

CHAPTER 4:

DEALING WITH INTERNAL DISTUR-BANCE

Understanding the way being and becoming can dance together opens up in-the-moment contentedness—what I feel as the rest of the Lord—as well as an availability to deep sanctification. In this section, we'll look in more detail at how holding both these views can facilitate our unfolding into the divine selves we already are.

RECAP OF BEING AND BECOMING

Just to jog the memory, the becoming (or doing) perspective is all about changing and transforming. It holds the truth that we aren't fully cooked yet and need time to become like God. In this mortal form, we are born into families, societies, and institutions that are wonderful as well as faulty. When we get messages from the outside world that something we say, think, or do is unacceptable or too much for those around us, we begin dividing unconsciously from our immediate, embodied experience. This is wise and intelligent as young people so that we can survive until adulthood—we need to stay acceptable to our caregivers so we can have love, food, and safety. However, as we trim down our sense of agency and forget to upgrade it when we become adults, the world can become very small to us. We live by old rules in a new world, and the mismatch can cause us chronic suffering and stunt our growth if not addressed. Whether it's through the gospel of Jesus Christ, other spiritual and contemplative practices, or simply the repetitive motion of life experience, we can eventually wake up to our stuckness and forge new paths in the alchemical process of the sanctification of our relative reality.

The being perspective is all about immediate and consistent okayness because of a deep trust that each moment, as it is, has everything we need to be in the rest of the Lord. We might sense we are living from this rest because our body sensations and feelings take on a certain backdrop of trust and ease, regardless of what's happening in the foreground. For some of us, this rest feels more like an open awareness, groundless ground, or womb of all existence. Indeed, we can find that we are already wrapped in divine light and love each moment of life.[1] The illusion that we are separate from God falls away, and each part of our experience can be met with kindness, completeness, and sacredness. This view is oftentimes lost in our becoming-centric society, and finding being can feel strange at first. If we go overboard on being, we lose contact with the reality of others' suffering and find it hard to take compassionate action. When balanced, being is the sense of wholeness from which we act, or don't, in each moment of our life for the good of all beings.

These two views can, at first, be experienced in isolation. With time, however, they begin to have a deeper and deeper relationship

1 John Kesler, *Integral Polarity Practice in Service of Leadership for Flourishing.*

with one another. Eventually, they find themselves entwining in a beautiful dynamic that brings both fully into each moment in appropriate ways—we find ourselves acting as and from the Mind of Christ, a mind of endless generosity, abundance, and peace.

WAKING UP TO OUR COSTLY STRATEGIES

In my experience, the biggest roadblock to living from a backdrop of wholeness is our habituated impulse to contract, shrink, or divide from experiential intensity. Something very primal in us can't seem to relax and open into the ocean of love and trust that is already here. Releasing this basic clenching against what's here is one of the most important things to practice in order to leave childhood maps of reactivity behind.

The first part of dealing with internal disturbance is usually a self-realization or confrontation. We come up against the same moment again and again, and the world feels like it's consistently working against us. Life feels so hard! We can even change settings, change partners, change church callings, or change our habits, but the chronic feelings of struggle and burnout remain.

Jesus said, "Let one who seeks not stop seeking until that person finds; and upon finding, the person will be disturbed; and being disturbed, will be astounded; and will reign over the entirety."[2]

At some point in my seeking life, I had to stop going outward to resolve the sense of chronic struggle in my life, and instead go far inward. What I found was incredibly disturbing. I turned toward myself—I came to my senses—and through that sensing found that the chasm of struggle was formed in my very own soul first. A fundamental division from my internal, immediate,

---

2 Gospel of Thomas, Saying 2.

and embodied experience started every moment on the wrong foot, so to speak.

You may experiment and find the same thing is true for you. However, many of us aren't ready to face this possibility. (Sometimes I still don't face it, even though part of me can never unknow it.) We continually seek a new program, supplement, spiritual practice, or teacher, hoping to resolve our chronic internal disturbances, but we never seem to get past them. Maybe reading this book is your attempt to go outward, again, to find relief. This is normal and healthy as we grow. Eventually, though, we might be invited to look at ourselves in a new way and feel our internal divisions spoiling every moment.

We realize that unconscious patterns of avoiding certain feelings, thoughts, or sensations have been guiding our lives for years. Much like someone becoming aware of wearing glasses that tint the real colors of each moment, we realize to a deeper and deeper degree that the origin of life's "struggle" is much closer than we'd guessed. True, we didn't place the glasses on our face, but that doesn't mean they're not there. Whether we like it or not, our early years as mortals give each of us a set of lenses through which to see the world, and we don't have much say in the set of glasses we get. Some spiritual traditions, the Latter-day Saints as well, say that some kind of lens, or veil of forgetfulness, falls on us as scales on our eyes. It's as if something is between us and a deeper reality.

Let's take Julian[3] for example. He's a middle-aged man who arrives in my office because of some troubling relationships in his life. His partner is too unappreciative and he's not sure how to get her to change. We work to understand what he feels and thinks in these moments, and it's clear he's quite upset. His feelings are real and he longs for more in the relationship. He comes to therapy to find gracious ways to invite his partner to be better, for his sake.

---

3 While the themes and conversations are real, all client names and revealing identifiers have been changed to respect client confidentiality.

As we continue talking, it turns out that his coworkers are also quite disappointing. They talk too much and too loudly, and their lunches are chronically smelly. He's had to quit a few jobs because of the people, always hoping the new setting will be better. Julian also has a habit of commenting on how my couch is not quite right for his body type, and he wonders if the temperature in the office can change sometimes.

I resonate with him on a lot of this. It's so hard to be married! And work can be very tough, especially if you can't pick your co-workers or what aromas come out of their lunch boxes. My couch is sometimes a little unimpressive to me as well, even though I thought it was perfect when I bought it earlier this year. In our sessions, it's usually easy for me to genuinely and openly validate, normalize, and reflect what he's going through. As we organize his experience, I ask him more about what he hopes to get from our work together:

Julian: I just wish people would be a little more considerate some-times, you know?

Paul: I do, and I can hear how troubling all of this is for you. I'm so glad you can be open with me about what it's really like to be you, on the inside.

J: Yeah, it felt really good to say all that. Like I just put down a heavy load.

P: Mmmmm (delighted sigh). Also, I hear that you do a lot to take care of yourself and advocate for what you need—even change a job if needed. Or talk to your wife, which can be tough. But even with all these efforts, it still seems like life isn't easing up for you. How do you deal with that?

J: I don't really know. Sometimes I get so confused. I know I'm supposed to trust in God and stuff, and read and pray, but I just don't know. It keeps on failing for me. I was kinda hoping you'd have the scoop on what's going on...

P: Yeah I hear that a lot in my line of work, "Just trust in God, it'll all work out," and then it doesn't seem to. That's strange.

I wonder if you'd be open to a little experiment, so we can learn a little more about what's going on here. Would you be up for that?

As a trained hypnotherapist, I frequently invite clients into new ways of relating to themselves, the world, and their problems. As we begin settling more intentionally into the embodied feeling of the moment, Julian confirms to me that the feelings in his body are consistent across multiple experiences. There's a chronic tightness in his stomach and a pursing of his lips and jaw. He's surprised to find out that this underlying body clenching is present in most of the troubling moments we've talked about so far, including work and marriage.

As we continue working, I help him feel his future inevitably unfolding if this same body tension continues coloring each moment. Having become so familiar with it, it's obvious to him that he'll probably keep reacting the same way he has in the past, as long as this tension backdrops the moment. We explore his future and find many moments when he's let himself or others down in some way. He even mentions that he's worried God will see him as a disappointment who didn't use his talents well and squandered his life away.

Julian begins to really realize both on an embodied and conceptual level that changing external circumstances in the future won't help him. Life around him isn't the full problem; he's forgotten the other half, which is him. It's the *inside Julian* that he carries everywhere he goes, filled with old protective strategies that interpret the moment and tell him what it is and how he needs to behave. With his adult faculties on hand, though, it's clear that these archaic methods won't do the job he has in mind for his future. He's waking up to the cost of continuing to live the way he had to as a younger person.

Since he cannot alter all of the external parts of life (the part of the problem he's been focusing on recently), we begin to explore how beneficial it can be to turn to the internal parts of him (the part of the problem he's not been able to work with yet). This internal layer includes how we *relate to* experience instead of the actual details and content of the experience.

This moment of waking up to our costly strategies is critical, and best held by both being and becoming viewpoints. The being viewpoint reassures him that where he is right now is workable, whole, and just right. He's right where he needs to be. And from this "just right" place, he can begin looking to see how to improve his way of relating to his daily life.

To my knowledge, without the being perspective really saturating someone's experience, the moment of waking up to our costly strategies can feel devastating, shameful, and discouraging. The being perspective is the warm and secure arms of Heavenly Parents who won't let go, no matter what we do, say, or are. Nothing can separate us from Their love. Our deepest nature, and every moment of our existence, is actually the same light that They are.

From here, working on becoming feels so different. No need to beat up the self, berate or criticize, or spend energy on anything outside of our unfolding becoming.

For Julian to update the way he relates to himself and the world around him, he will need to practice, intentionally, allowing certain sensations and states of mind instead of avoiding them, which he usually does by complaining and criticizing the people around him. Shifting this pattern will allow him to build a life based around what he most deeply values instead of a life based on avoiding what disturbances he cannot handle in his experience. When he is no longer divided internally from his experience, an inner union and settledness can stabilize as his default backdrop to life experience.

THE "THEN WHAT?" APPROACH

One short practice you can do to help yourself see your costly strategies is to ask yourself, "Then what?" when you feel stuck in life. Remember, costly strategies are those we employ to avoid certain internal experiences, leading us to cut off decision pathways. Maybe a decision is coming at you and you're not sure what to do...

> *Gosh, I don't know if I should go to that ward function tomorrow night. I promised I would... I feel like I should, but do I really have the energy?*
>
> If I don't, though, what will others think?
>
> *Yeah but if I do go, I'll just have to put on a face the whole time and I'd so much rather be home.*
>
> You mean this dump? Look at all these chores you haven't done. You wanna be here??
>
> *Dang, yeah there's no way this place feels relaxing and nourishing. I wonder if I can just show up for a little bit?*
>
> But we still have to make the casserole, right? That's one of the worst parts of going—making something for it. And it's gonna add to this pigsty!
>
> *Jeez, maybe I won't go after all. But. I promised I would...*

As you can see, most of us loop like this, endlessly circling our minivan around the same cul-de-sac—we put on some serious mental and emotional miles, but don't actually get anywhere.

This is where the question, "Then what?" is helpful. Don't let your mind circle back around. Keep it moving forward:

Gosh, I don't know if I should go to that ward function tomorrow night. I feel like I should, but do I really have the energy?

If I don't, though, what will—WAIT. I need to do that exercise from the book. What was it again? Oh yeah, "Then what?"

Well, if I don't go, I'll get stuck here. At home. Again, and see all this mess.

Yes. And then what?

Hmpf. When I see all this mess, I'll feel horrible and just wanna burn it all down.

Yes. And then what?

Then, I don't actually burn it down, but I feel a lot of shame and self-loathing! I mean come on, I can't do that!

Yes but what if you do? And then what?

Well, I feel self-loathing, I overeat and stay up too late trying to numb out on Tik Tok, and then I wake up feeling horrible.

Yes. And then what?

Then I mope around and eventually take a shower and try to act like an adult again.

Yes. And then what?

Well, life keeps going and I take my kids to school.

Okay. Now we know what's down that path.

More often than not, our aversion to letting our mind play out the full story is due to a seriously disturbing interior experience just around the corner. In our subconscious logic, it's better to circle the cul-de-sac a few more times than to drive down the road and face our unpleasant inner sensations. In this case, it's probably the intense sensations in the body around shame and self-loathing that we're avoiding.

In the above example, we could do the same exercise for *going* to the ward function scenario instead of *staying home*, but we will find a similar situation: That path leads to a serious internal disturbance that we don't want or aren't sure how to face. You wouldn't be alone in thinking that this process feels difficult. Know that you're fighting a lot of unconscious momentum that tries to pretend like these negative states don't exist. It's common for my clients to have *no idea* what to say when I ask "Then what?" It's as if their mind has never had to go there. Because it hasn't.[4]

Asking "Then what?" encourages us to locate our troubling internal state. Sometimes we're averse because that path leads to consequences both likely and harmful—like someone getting sick or dying. Even then, we still find our internal self clenching against that perceived future disturbance, and it clouds our capacity to have full agency. It doesn't have to be that way.

When we complete the "Then what?" activity and take the experience all the way to the end of the line, we clarify what exactly we're averse to: intense internal experience. When we aren't trained to or supported in facing these disturbances, we have no option but to keep the endless aversion going. Knowing how to face disturbance completely changes this internal circling—if handling internal disturbance is possible, we just jump the hurdle and keep going.

This activity also reveals that both paths include disturbance. We cannot escape it. I go to the ward activity and face disturbance; I stay home, and face disturbance. My experience has shown me that instead of pretending like we can pick a non-disturbing path, it's simply better to learn to deal with disturbance in our immediate, embodied experience.[5] Once we can pay that price, consistently, the world opens up.

---

4 Also, please note that this exercise can quickly lead to someone feeling invalidated, not seen, or emotionally disregarded. Safety, close attunement, and a deep sensitivity are essential if someone is asking you to lead them in this exercise.

5 Other useful psychological and meditative approaches focus on beliefs and cognitions, as well, but I've found that sensation as the focus of disturbance is the most potent way through. Including a list of beliefs or themes that trigger the sensory disturbance is helpful as well, but working through it, in my experience, is best done on a raw, sensory level. Here is a great scientific study my teacher Thomas shared with me on why the most basic sensation-level focus may be helpful: Laukkonen & Slagter, "From many to (n)one: Meditation and the plasticity of the predictive mind." https://doi.org/10.1016/j.neubiorev.2021.06.021

When someone has mastered the skill of feeling their disturbances, the above scenario goes like this:

I don't go to the activity.

I see my house and feel revolted. I begin to shame and loathe myself.

*I open up, unguardedly, to the sensation-level intensity of the dis-
turbance, and it passes, or doesn't, but I'm not blocked from enjoying
the next activity.*

*I continue my evening however I please, guided by my highest, most
sacred self.*

That's it. Easier said than done, for sure. But that's where
practice comes in.

PRACTICING OUTSIDE THE MOMENT

After waking up to our strategies of dividing from or avoiding our
disturbing internal experience, it's time to update our model for
making decisions in the world. Especially in this initial phase,
I highly recommend practicing opening to disturbance (which
is how we resolve our internal divisions) in a safe, controlled
environment. Practice usually starts in ideal settings—like a
therapist's office, retreat center, quiet home, or other supportive
space—and then gradually moves into more and more disruptive,
chaotic settings, until we can finally face disturbance in real time,
in real life moments.

We'll look at practicing outside the moment first, and then
move into integrating practice into daily living.

A frequent first step in exploring disturbance is actually to
find stability. Much like settling the body and balance before
entering tree pose in yoga, we can start by feeling our own two

---

Other psychotherapy practices, like Somatic Experiencing, seem to agree on the benefit
of focusing on sensation in transformative experiences.

feet on the ground. You might already have a centering practice that works for you—use that. It could be journaling, a hot drink, a supportive partner, breathing practices, meditation, prayer, or transformative imagery. Anything that brings you to your center will work.

From here, we begin to invite disruption. As in Chapter 2, regarding freeing up our agency, we begin to find an edge to our capacities. When practicing outside the moment, feel free to slowly introduce non-present stimuli to activate the body and mind. You might imagine a scene that brings mild discomfort. Hear something related to it and/or just let the body begin feeling a sensation that has longed to come forward.

Again, I've found that it's most helpful to deal with sensations when practicing. If finding sensations is difficult, allow yourself to wade into it slowly. A lot of us have ideas, thoughts, and beliefs popping up:

> *There's no way I can do this.*
> *I can't even look at so-and-so's face again.*
> *Even the idea of that moment makes me retch inside.*

These thoughts are great gateways into your emotional experience. Let the thoughts unveil the emotions to you:

Sadness: Usually a result of some sort of loss. Are your thoughts connected to loss?

Anger: A sign of injustice occurring. Have you or someone you care for been wronged?

Fear: A sense that you are about to experience pain or harm. "Pay attention!" the body says.

Joy: A sense of liberation, connection, and Yes. Is something inside wanting this?

Each emotion has a kind of somatic map. Like a constellation of stars, sensations combine into a bigger shape that we call emotion. So, look at the map in the body. Where is it tight/loose? Heavy/light? Open/closed? Energized/numb?

From here, really try to locate one or two of the strongest sensations. I recommend starting slow and trying to stay with a sensation for about 30-60 seconds. Commit yourself to the task first, then start a timer or gaze at a clock. With all your concentration and mindfulness, stay with all of the sensation. Don't abandon any aspect of the moment. Give your animal body the reins. Let it run as it wills in terms of sensation moving in the body. Let it have its way with you.

To be clear, this is often very intense for people. You may have thoughts that try to distract you or old patterns of subtle avoidance appearing. It takes practice to allow intensity to course through you. It's okay to take it slowly. Trust that you will have everything you need as you continue moving forward.

Also, note that this complete openness to the developing sensations is not about acting it out. There is no intention to validate the ideas, actions, or morality of the experience that *initiated* the disturbance, only an openness to the moment *at the level of body sensations*. We aren't saying that if you feel rage in your body, the attending sensations should be free to manifest in the world in any way they want, which might include hurting someone or something. It's quite the opposite, actually.

This process is about allowing the energy of these moments to flow freely through your experience without your intervention in mitigating, shifting, or altering them in any way. Sit with the unmovable, unshakable steadfastness of a mountain that remains amidst rain, fire, snow, and wind. Sensations come and go, you remain.

Additionally, sometimes the sensations in the body do want to release via a physical action like pounding, shaking, or yelling. These are okay as well, and I invite you to check in if there are other people in the physical space beforehand to see if they invite your expression and release of the intensity of disturbance. You may find that these kinds of release moments are best practiced with a professional who has training in the area first, before engaging in the practice on your own. Check in with your trained professional to see if there's wisdom regarding sitting with it versus moving with it.

As I said, this practice is best started in small doses, 30-60 seconds each. Many people I work with start with 5-15 seconds. Do what you can. Every moment you engage your sensations here is a long-term investment in your highest self abiding in its fullest agency.

Begin to notice what happens to you and your sensations, as you sit in this way with them. Do they intensify? Soften? Change locations? Stay with sensations as best you can, devoid of concepts, meaning, or stories about them.

After the time ends, return to stability, if the practice didn't already spontaneously bring you there. Feel the ground beneath and through you, and center again as needed. Congratulate your-self—you've completed your first round of dissolving internal division. You are "more Ziony" than before, and you are still just as good and whole. The miracle of your inner transformation is here.

This process can be completed as frequently or infre-quently as needed.

PRACTICING INSIDE THE MOMENT

After repeated success in allowing more sensory disturbance into our experience, we can begin using the same skills in real time. Before in-the-moment practice, I suggest starting in settings intended to hold a safe container for your experience. When this feels consistently doable, you can begin altering the environment in ways that are less and less supportive to your process until you can do it in any setting.

I'll use a therapy office setting as the starting point and lay out a possible map of building more and more autonomy.

First, a client and I will practice in my office for several sessions until there is a familiarity with the process and consistent success in delving into sensations and then back to stable ground. This doesn't have to include every aspect of their life, but just enough of life that there are a few topics and themes where this practice consistently works.

For example, if a mother of two kids comes to therapy for anxiety management, she might describe her world getting smaller and smaller because of having to avoid things that bring up her anxiety. We might practice staying with the disturbing experience of her body sensations that often arise just before, during, or after anxiety-inducing moments. I'd help her imagine a screaming child, a messy kitchen, or a babysitter dropping out at the last moment. Then we'd find the sensations that come to her, commit not to pull away from them, allow them to move around in her experience, realize they won't damage her, and then return to stable ground again.

After she can practice this way consistently in my office and with my guidance, I may invite her to do the process in my office without my verbal assistance. She'll close her eyes for a couple of minutes, complete the practice, and then open them again and report what's happened. We'll tune up anything that needs tuning up and then practice again.

When she's comfortable on her own in my office, I might ask her to practice in her car in the parking lot, just before our next session starts. This allows her to try it out in a new setting, but with the assurance that she'll see me in the next ten minutes if she has trouble with it. After this is successful, I'll invite her to do it several hours before a session instead of ten minutes before one. I might also give her a recording of me guiding her into and out of the experience, to help her access the full practice at home, whenever she likes.

Next, she might pick more settings that begin to get closer to the actual moment. She might try it at home when her kids are out of the house, or after putting them to bed. Then she could practice when they are in the home, but with her partner in the next room, where she can hear them. Or she can practice alone in a messy kitchen, feeling the overwhelm that comes to her with the daunting tasks around her.

Eventually, after so many rounds, a new pattern is forming more consistently where she doesn't turn away from the difficulty of her immediate, embodied experience. She's proven again and again that it doesn't harm her, and she doesn't have to keep avoiding tasks that are connected to the arising of unsettling feelings and sensations inside. (This is the gift of the being skill; you are able to sit with the in-the-moment experience, saying Yes to what is.)

This pattern can naturally flow into everyday moments, where now she intentionally opens herself up to the difficult sensations she has *in the moment* of parenting, or overwhelm, or disappointment. Everything in her past urges her to find a way to escape, numb out, distract, or annihilate the "cause" of internal disruption. Now, she holds the intensity with a deeper, more mature capacity that doesn't require her to abandon what she cares about most. (She is becoming a different kind of parent now, seeing her skills increase over time, improving on the internal conditions she wanted to change.)

She begins having breakthrough moments.[6] Her child has a tantrum about a meal or a clothing choice. Her stomach clenches, her jaw tightens, and her face feels like it's bursting. She allows the sensations, takes a breath, and feels the ground beneath her as well as the intense sensations. Sensations swell. She remains, held by a sense of wholeness and acceptance of everything happening

---

6 Please note that this process has its own timeline for each person. Especially in those who have experienced childhood trauma, there are often additional layers that can be handled with more intensive trauma treatments. Oftentimes blocks to this "facing disturbance" process reveal where we need to spend extra time in order for practices like this to land in the body and soul.

to her. She experiences both the intensity of the sensations as well as the reality of her highest intentions in the moment: To be there for her child, just as she has been here for herself in all this practicing.

Virtuous actions spill out of her, even in the midst of her intensity. She moves into comfort, nurturing, support, encouragement, or whatever else the moment calls for. New patterns around her internal and external child are taking shape. She now knows that internal disturbance is not a factor that has to dictate the actions she takes in life.

There aren't any bitter cups that she won't drink on the path of her divine motherhood journey. She's a Savior on Mount Zion, and she carries Zion within her. She hasn't had to strong-arm herself here, either, but has found a way to feel whole along the way.

She's becoming perfected, while being whole.

Let's Check In:

Our ability to face difficulty is often closely related to our access to support, resources, and grounding. The deeper the grounding and stability, the more we can risk facing the intensity of our internal disturbances (in the form of thoughts, feelings, and especially body sensations).

If the background of being whole ever falters, our ability to face difficulty drops as well. Sometimes we feel like the background of being and the foreground of becoming switch places, or one might disappear entirely. My experience is that when being disappears from the backdrop, I'm consumed and overtaken by the difficulties of disturbance—I'm compromised and unable to meet them with kindness or acceptance, and I find myself dividing from my experience in an effort to escape the intensity.
(See image on next page.)

Imagine how you sit with a 450-pound gorilla when it's behind its glass at the zoo; now imagine how your attitude changes when it's out of its exhibit, staring you in the face. The better the container, the more we can allow, embrace, and celebrate gorillas being gorillas.

big wholeness allows big anger without overwhelming the system	tiny wholeness only allows tiny anger (any more and it overwhelms the system)	if anger ever switches to background, it usually overwhelms the system; internal division kicks in to protect self from intensity

THE EVOLVING SENSE OF SELF

Something else happens when we consistently drink the bitter cups placed before us in life. Who we are—and what we are—evolves and refines.

It's common to feel like we are predominantly our physical existence: maybe I'm my profession, I'm my BMI, I'm my bolo tie, I'm my hairdo, I'm my kid's behavior in public, I'm the number in my bank account. When put bluntly like that, most of us can refute that and say we're not that shallow. But, on second thought, I'm sure glad I'm not wearing *that guy's* shirt and tie to church, yikes! And thank goodness I don't do *that* for a living. I'm so glad my wife is *this* and not *that*. And there's no way you're touching my money.

As you can see, we might be more identified with the physical stuff of our lives than we like to admit. And that's okay. It's quite normal, and healthy to a degree, as we learn to shift what we identify with.

In my observation, when we commit to follow the gospel of Jesus Christ, we usually end up caring less and less about physical things over time. We take care of ourselves, but don't overly stress about our looks or belongings. We have sufficient for our needs, but we realize they aren't the actual substance of our happiness.

As disciples, we also don't get too ruffled when our emotions arise. Pain, anger, pleasure, joy, embarrassment, mistakes, successes. We can *have* all of these experiences instead of these experiences *having us*. Disturbances happen, and we remain.

Eventually, we begin to realize that we aren't as finite, localized, or bound as we thought. Physical attributes change, locations and scenery shift, our emotions rise and fall, disturbance rages and abates, and something is still *here*. It's the *us* that remains, no matter what changes.

A feeling of liberation comes over us, and we become more transparent and more impactful at the same time. We are a flowing pattern of sensations and thoughts and beliefs that shift in different contexts, while a part of us remains the same over every context. We feel the being and becoming parts in their togetherness. Our capacity to be vessels for good shifts, and more light seems to come through as our availability for non-egoic action is sustained across more and more contexts.

We start to realize we're not *doing* all of the stuff that we're doing. God pours out of our heart, voice, face, and body. We become no one in the sense that we are unblocked from the light pouring through, but we become the most important someone as well, since we are God's hands on earth in only the exact way we can be right now.

As this process continues over and over, an inseparable union is realized and we remember that we are sealed forever as God, birthing every moment continually. It becomes vital that we completely disappear to let God through, and also vital that we become something more substantial in this life to walk always in sacred beauty.[7]

---

7 John Kesler, *Integral Polarity Practice in Service of Leadership for Flourishing.*

TRUST FALL

Our resolving of internal division, our evolving sense of divine self, and our awakened wholeness can give the sense that we are just flowing, joyfully surrendered, through life. A transcendent trust emerges where we know not the hour of His coming, nor where our next meal comes from, sometimes even literally, yet an abiding trust pervades our experience.

We begin to trust not only that the sun will rise in the morning or that the world will still exist when we blink and reopen our eyes, but that the very next sacred moment will unfold in just the right way. And we'll be along for the ride. In fact, we might be part of the ride!

It's powerful.

Trust enlivens the powerful faith of someone who knows how to midwife the next moment into existence, over and over again, without effort, and sometimes with strenuous effort, for the benefit of all. It can be so terrifying not to know the next sentence to come out, yet to open the mouth and trust that Divinity is flowing.

"The bad news is you're falling through the air, nothing to hang on to, no parachute. The good news is there's no ground."[8]

"When you are transformed, the world is transformed. For you are the world, and the world is you."[9]

"Here now, begins the journey beyond union, beyond self and God, a journey into the silent and still regions of the Unknown."[10]

---

8 Chögyam Trungpa Rinpoche

9 Mary Magdalene, The Gospel of Mary.

10 Bernadette Roberts, *The Experience of No-Self: A Contemplative Journey.*

PART III: THE LATTER-DAY SAINT PATH

I've sprinkled into this book various Latter-day Saint themes, examples, and scriptures so far, but let's really get into the heart of a few key elements of Church doctrine and culture. We'll look at how eternal partnership and our local wards can be crucibles for our being and becoming. We'll also end with a delightful section with guest authors riffing on wholeness in their own gospel lives.

CHAPTER 5:

DISTURBANCE IN AN ETERNAL PARTNERSHIP

Thus far, we've mostly focused on how to search the individual self for disturbance and re-relate to it in ways that make it non-problematic. Now, we'll begin looking at how disturbance is activated in relational moments.

ETERNITY INVITES SURRENDER

You may resonate with a common human feeling: being stuck. Take, for example, the moment you realize who will be sitting next to you on your plane trip for the next three and a half hours. Or, who plops down next to you on the bus commute to work. Some of us have thought, "Jeez, let's get this ride over with asap. I don't want to see/smell/hear/feel this person next to me."

Now, consider the dynamic in a common Latter-day Saint marriage—partners for *eternity*. Being stuck with someone on public transit is one thing, and comes with the hopeful promise of a short duration. Eternal partnership, on the other hand, completely skips the pretending or fantasy that there's an exit.

In a forever partnership, you lock it up and toss out the keys. No exits, no endings, no escape.

For some, that's a scary thing. Certainly, there are always ways to end a marriage, and probably many circumstances where it's healthy and important to do so. I'm not saying here that all couples should stay together or part ways. Abusive relationships are real, and many are stuck emotionally, financially, and physically in terrible partnerships. I believe that leaving those types of situations is appropriate. For myself, I experience my wife, Anna, to have good intentions even when she upsets me, so I feel confident in choosing to stay. Not everyone can say they are with someone who has good intentions, so some of this section may not apply to all couples. For our purposes here, though, I'll explore how eternal partnership can offer a compelling place for confronting our disturbances.

As noted earlier, we developed early strategies to avoid our most core vulnerabilities and stay cared for as young people. We divided internally from our immediate experience as children because we didn't have the adult capacities required to trust, hold, and allow the fullness of our experiential intensity. Eternal partnership, and partnership in general, is often one of the best places to bring up and consistently activate our disturbances.

The astonishing reality is that our partners, just by being themselves every day, are going to activate our internal disturbances.[1] In the world of pain and disturbance, bad intentions aren't even required. In fact, many of us have great intentions for ourselves and partners, and still the turmoil remains. Two people with great intentions, in continual close proximity, will

---

1 Bruce Tift, *Already Free.*

nudge each other's tender spots and deeply disrupt idealistic hopes of constant comfort.

And that's totally okay. Sometimes there are partnerships that don't come with daily or hourly disturbances, but for the majority of humans I know, disturbance is a daily medicine in partnership. Oftentimes we think that a disruption in our inner experience is a sign that something is bad or not going well, but as we open with kindness to all experience, we can begin to realize that disturbance is just one facet of the many-sided jewel of life.

Eternal partnership can create conditions for growth. Instead of trying to find an exit or an easy way forward, we may eventually come to ourselves and decide to face ourselves on a new, inner level. It's my experience that there are some lessons that cannot be learned by bowing out, easing up, or changing scenery. When we commit to staying in the discomfort beyond our initial reaction to pull away, we are able to more clearly see our strategies of avoidance that have created the inner division described in previous chapters. We find that we consistently turn away from the truth of our immediate experience.

STARTING WITH THE END IN MIND

A key tenet of divine partnership is that it enables a Godly becoming that eventually mirrors God's own current reality. The God life is a life of partnership, union, oneness, and boundless creation and destruction throughout time and eternity.

After marriage, there's not much on the Latter-day gospel checklist. Certainly, a lot of change, transformation, and meaningful service happens in enduring to the end, but the entire structure of our celestial home is actually already in place. From what the Church currently teaches, even Saints in their early twenties can have "all the pieces" in place that will carry them into the eternities.

Since most twenty-year-olds I know don't seem fully cooked, in the Godhood sense, it makes me wonder how we can approach partnership with the eternal end in mind. It's almost like giving an eight-year-old a concert grand piano for their birthday, along with a stage and auditorium. Everything is set for greatness, and kids can make beautiful sounds at any age, yet something still needs to happen for certain kinds of greatness to echo through the hall.

The perfect scaffolding of partnership is like the piano and auditorium, and facing our disturbance in relationships is the daily deliberate practice required to make celestial sound waves. In one sense, there's really nothing to do or change—it's all here! On the other hand, there is so much to do, with no real end in sight.

Something about starting couples off with their complete divine structures tells me that *how we attend* to the relational dynamic of marriage changes everything. Let's look at how we can attend to our relationship in internal and external ways.

CODEPENDENCY WITH PARTNER

There's a buzzword I've heard floating around regarding relationships: codependent. I'm not actually sure what each person means when they use that word, but for our purposes, we can define it as any time we get stuck in singular views like these:

1) Our partner is the only cause of our internal disturbance, and/or

2) Our partner is the only solution to our internal disturbance.

As you can see, codependency is often a way to try and outsource the problem of and solution to our inner experience. We can get stuck trying to solve an internal problem with an external object or person. This is an inherently difficult route to internal peace because it requires the actions of people and things we can't control. It limits agency and makes us solely "things to be acted upon."[2] From a wholeness perspective, there's nothing wrong with being acted upon, as long as the other option of acting is also available to us. However, frequently in a codependent dynamic, one possibility is dominant and the other is absent.

Imagine walking down a hallway which ends in two doors. If we have agency, both doors will be accessible and open to us, and we can choose one based on our value or preference in the moment. A codependent dynamic, however, is a hallway that ends in one open door and one locked door. We can only be acted upon by our partner, completely at the mercy of their behavior, instead of also being able to act.

The power center of codependency is also important—it's almost always away from ourselves and toward something or someone else. This external locus of focus, or control, makes honoring our immediate, embodied experience very difficult. Frequently, looking outside ourselves is an easy way to get out of our intense sensations, feelings, and thoughts. Sometimes looking outward is life-changing and expands our sense of being, as well as our love of all humanity. But, especially early on, it's just one more way we abandon ourselves and our internal experience. When we find ourselves stuck in codependent dynamics, it simply means we haven't learned how to land in the power of our own agency. As infants, power was outside of us and our only option was to be dependent (external locus of control). As we mature emotionally, we can also access independence (internal locus of control), opening both doors of agency for the first time.[3]

If we go too far into independence, though, we can cut ourselves off from the meaningful option of depending on one

---

2 D&C 58:27-28

3 This sense of control and agency continues on a very interesting trajectory, but for our purposes, opening both doors on the moment will suffice.

another. I do believe we are wired, spiritually and biologically, to want, need, and long for connection via relationship. It seems to be a primary nutrient that cannot really be replaced by anything else. I fully encourage vulnerable sharing, embracing each other in our deepest moments, and advocating for what we need. All of those steps, however, usually require some level of self-knowledge, self-confrontation, and self-acceptance in order for us to take the next step. Many of us don't have the skills to do the inner job, so we start learning that process with someone who is willing to help us organize, validate, and honor our internal experiences. For some of us, this mentorship happens as young people, and we emerge into adulthood knowing how to sense, honor, and respond to our inner experience. Many of us, though, haven't learned how to hold our experience in its fullness and tend to outsource responsibility for our inner disturbances.

I'm a supporter of repairing, healing, and completing the attachment loops of our past. It is often through being held by others that we learn to hold ourselves more fully. As we are held, we can hold more, and as we hold more of ourselves, we can hold more for others.[4] In therapy-speak, I'm a supporter of both co-regulation and self-regulation, and I encourage my clients to develop healthy versions of both. However, the focus of this book is more around how individuals can take responsibility for their own wholeness.

The codependency that I'm trying to point out is usually accompanied by a divided internal posture, something like self-disgust, self-ignorance, or self-avoidance. As such, no amount of external factors lining up or going our way will actually bring us what we really want and need in a lasting way. That can only come when we stop leaving ourselves. It begins when we give up the fantasy that others are responsible for our internal experience.

---

4 For interpersonal practice, something like Emotionally-Focused Couples therapy or Gottman's couples resources can be helpful. I was also really impacted by Dan Brown's Three Pillars approach outlined in *Attachment Disturbances in Adults: Treatment for Comprehensive Repair*.

This can be a tough pill to swallow, but in a supportive environment, it can be healthy to begin facing ourselves internally. *What is activating in myself, simply from my partner being themselves?* Frequently, we feel like our partners are *causing* the disturbance we are feeling, when in reality they are usually just igniting something already present. The internal machinery was there before we arrived in the relationship, and them just being themselves happens to activate it very consistently. We usually want to blame them because they were the closest in proximity to us when we got activated. But, in reality, *something inside us* is activating, the origin of which they probably didn't participate in.

Practice

It is common in partnership for someone to get triggered or activated. This could be anything from a partner leaving their smoothie cup out to dry, spending money in ways you don't agree with, smelling a certain way, or even looking at you in "just that way."

When this happens, it's again important to ask ourselves: **What inner experience is activated in me right now? Am I trying to avoid a sensation, or perhaps considering it problematic?** Can you find it, again, like the practice we did earlier? What thoughts, feelings, and sensations are present now? Can you find a way to hold them with kindness, instead of turning away or acting to numb them? I usually recommend doing this outside of the moment, as I shared before: Even now, you can think about or jot down a few times where you are consistently disturbed by your partner. Let your mind's focus go from your partner's behavior back to you. What thoughts, feelings, and sensations are here?

> If you find yourself thinking about them again, come to your senses. Literally come back to the senses (feeling, seeing, hearing) you are having in this disturbance. In particular, see what raw sensations seem loudest.
>
> Repeating our practice before, set a timer for 60 seconds and just let the full sensory experience unfold. Don't pull away from yourself; stay. Things come and go, and you remain. Feel your inner workings trying to make sense and adapt to a new pattern of staying with your disturbance. Notice if any resistance, rebuttals, or beliefs come up.

What if you began living as if your partner wasn't the cause or solution to your disturbances? What if the energy that usually goes out to your partner (often in the form of blame or coercion) stayed with you, in a more positive form, to help you be with your difficult sensations? Does this new stance bring fruits of agency and liberation or fruits of victimization and entrapment?

What if you accepted that your partner will always disturb you on some level? Or that no matter how perfectly they try to console you, you'll always still need something else from them? (Again, these questions are only for partnerships of mutual respect and good intentions. I don't recommend tolerating abuse of any kind.)

These questions are often extremely disturbing to consider. Sometimes, they begin to wear away some of the fantasies or stories we tell ourselves about our condition. When the narrative falls away, we are left bare to the stark realities the stories were keeping us safe from. I'm not saying this will work for everyone, but I hope that experience teaches what's working. If you adopt some of these ideas, will you be able to live more in accordance with your highest sense or purpose, or not?

THE FANTASY OF CONTINUATION

So far, I've framed an eternal marriage as something that encourages us to give up the option for exit. That's true. As I've experienced eternal marriage, it's brought me to confront myself further than ever before. However, sometimes the framing of an LDS marriage—eternal and everlasting—can do the opposite of inviting us to face our disturbance. It may create barriers to living in the reality that *partnership can end at any time, for any reason.* The common adage of "take it for granted" expresses this pitfall well; we may assume that our marriage is solid, lasting, and independent of our influence. It's simply granted that we're in partnership forever, so we can casually hold on to unhealthy habits and dynamics because "let's face it, partner—you're not going anywhere. We're stuck forever."

Perhaps a personal story can help illustrate this.[5] When I first met Anna, my wife, we began talking a lot about what it means to love someone unconditionally versus romantically. We both came into the relationship with our share of healthy and not-so-healthy love and wanted to really smooth it out in our relationship together.

As we grew closer, the phrase "I love you" became a fitting and beautiful way to express what we were feeling toward each other. However, it didn't quite point to the uniqueness of what we were hoping to give and bring to one another. We both realized that we could love, and fall in love with, many kinds of people. The *love* aspect wasn't difficult, but something about *choosing* each other, regardless of the ease or difficulty of the relationship, had more of the flavor we were hoping to savor in marriage.

To verbally share "I choose you" became the real magic moment for us. Inviting the *choice* aspect of our partnership also brought up the polar, ever-present opposite, "I don't choose you." And, when we nakedly see the reality of any relationship,

---

5 My wife has graciously consented to my sharing the following details of our dynamic.

we discover an obvious, yet very disturbing and inconvenient truth: Our partner can stop choosing us. At any time, for any reason, this can all go away.[6] Just like that. In addition, we can also stop choosing our partner, at any time, for any reason. This is the nature of our mortal, physical relationships, even after temple promises.

Instead of pretending that we had a great relationship and it would last forever and ever, Anna and I began leaning into the reality that it could, and still can, end any second. And, it's our individual and joint choosing of each other and the relationship that is actually sustaining it, moment to moment. For many of us, resting in this risky reality is deeply unsettling, so we'll strategize and rationalize all sorts of behaviors instead of facing this truth. Sometimes "trusting" the sealing ordinance is actually an act of avoidance, a weak wish that we'll magically just start treating each other in a celestial way with no work or personal disturbance required. What happens, instead, when we open both doors of agency fully? We can say: I can be here, or not. My partner can choose me, or not.

I often invite clients to speak the very same words:

"At any time, for any reason, I can stop choosing this relationship. At any time, for any reason, my partner can stop choosing this relationship."[7]

---

6 I will use the phrase "for any reason" many times in this section. The reality of my experience shows me that bounds on our agency are quite different that we assume; we feel much less or maybe much more free than we actually are. Maybe we call this boundless flavor radical agency. Many people during a therapy session say that they "can't" do something, like not feed their kids, not have sex with their partner, not turn off their phone, not speak up, etc. The feeling of impossibility is real, but they can actually do all of those things. There are consequences, but the reason they don't do it is not because they "can't" from an agent perspective. It's usually because the consequences are incredibly painful or misaligned with their intentions.

The phrase "for any reason" is to clarify that the "can't" stories we tell ourselves are actually fake news. They aren't related to agency, but rather related to our limiting self-beliefs, frequently informed by past pain. When we say, I "can't," we reveal internal, sensation-based brick walls that when pushed on, crumble right through. My hope is that this phrase helps us all reveal where we pretend we don't have agency, not so that we do all the unhealthy things we think we "can't," but so that we're actually able to choose "can" when it matters most.

7 Note that this phrase is emphasizing the agentic side of a relationship (personal responsibility and choice), as opposed to the communal or relational side of a partnership

Depending on the personal background of the client, some variation of this can be profound:

"No matter how hard I try, or how much I get right, my partner can stop choosing this relationship."

These potent phrases blast through the stories we tell ourselves. Verbalizing the free-fall of relationship also releases all of the stuck energy that is being used to keep the risky reality at bay. When we come into authentic relationship with the true circumstances of partnership, we can begin living into the dynamic with greater acceptance, vulnerability, and responsibility. Only after fully accepting that we can end it at any time can we also fully choose to continue it.

Please note that in saying these phrases, we aren't at all *moving* in a certain direction. We aren't taking big action with this exercise; it's for the inner chambers first. It's about confronting the subtle mental and emotional content that is clogging up agentic, authentic relationship.[8]

When faced with the idea of *not choosing the relationship* or *not being chosen by their partner*, some people are so nervous that they cannot say it. One side is blocked, fully. Again, in my experience, agency includes the full opening of a choice. Both doors must be accessible and open—good and evil, pleasure and pain, virtue and vice. When we look deeply into the moment, we find that we always have a choice. And, when we have a choice, and *choose partnership*, the authenticity of our choice feels radically different.

(we need to take care of each other). Both sides are important, but since most couples are coming into therapy to work on communicating, connecting with each other, or resolving some sort or issue together, they are already supposing and leaning into the relational side, in my clinical experience. Sometimes, however, it is also important to invite the relational phrase, "At any time, for any reason, I can fully give myself to my partner, completely unguarded." Or, "No matter how hard/little I try, or how much I get right/wrong, my partner may completely commit to, and give themselves fully, to me." The possibilities for these jolting phrases are endless.

8 Another interesting note is that choosing to stay or go in a relationship can happen from an intention to avoid or embrace the immediate, embodied intensity of our reality. I can never guess which intention someone is acting from, so I find it's best simply to ask the person if I need to know, instead of assuming.

Currently, this "I choose you" practice feels two-fold for me: First, I remember and connect with my long-term intention to be in forever partnership with Anna. (I currently hold this to be a sacred way to live my life.) Second, I fully inhabit the present moment, noticing all that she is, wants, feels, needs, desires, delights in, etc. and release myself to this momentary relational union, saying, "I choose you. I choose this." I try to remain unguarded, while accepting that I can never be fully there, consistently, and will most likely always need to remember and return to this sensibility for the rest of my life.

It's an eternal practice because it holds a forever perspective, and it's an eternal practice because it's happening in every moment, most likely forever. When these micro and macro motions sync up, I find that I'm continually disturbed by my marriage with Anna, and continually blessed. Life is rich, mundane, complex, simple, dynamic—expanding and contracting in a rhythm of continual flow. Ironically, when we confront the fantasy of eternal continuation head-on, we find the daydream disappears, yet our ability to sustain relationships increases.[9]

Practice

Try this for yourself. First, sense your thoughts, feelings, and body sensations. Then, say out loud:

"No matter what I do, at any time, for any reason, my partner can stop choosing this relationship." *And/or*

"No matter what's going on, at any time, for any reason, I can stop choosing this relationship."[10]

---

9 Please note that I'm not commenting on the "fantasy of continuation" from a gospel doctrine perspective, meaning I'm not saying the sealing ordinance is bunk. I mean this from an internal, emotional, and somatic withholding that prevents us from being fully present to our partnership in the dynamic. It's a belief that protects us from the raw intensity of vulnerability and the possibility of relational pain—at any time for any reason. Like closing our eyes when we are about to witness a car crash, we go dark to reality, hindering our capacity to be in a relationship in life's next moment.

10 If it's more potent for you, try the alternate phrase, "At any time, for any reason, I can fully give myself to my partner, completely unguarded." or "At any time, for any

What thoughts, feelings, and sensations are present now?

Let the full sensory experience unfold. Don't pull away from yourself. Stay. Things come and go, and you remain. Feel your inner workings trying to make sense and adapt to reality again. Notice if any resistance, rebuttals, or beliefs come up.

Often, our partner can feel our subtle withholding in the relationship. It's as if we're not fully in the room, available to what's here. If you discover new information about how you hold your side of the relationship, you may consider sharing that with your partner. It can often be very validating and connecting to bring our authentic self-confrontation to the partnership, in the spirit of relating authentically to one another. If you can, state what you're learning about yourself simply, kindly, and without much explanation or wordiness. Let the impact of your words be the power, not your explanations, caveats, or sharing of context. If you feel personally resourced, trust that you can both have a complete experience together.

THE CRUCIBLE IS HERE

Eternal marriage could be the Latter-day monastery. In our time, it's less common for people to take up spiritual living as a full-time endeavor. The Church is rare in this regard because it supports things like full-time missionary and temple service. So, you're probably ahead of the crowd in terms of knowing what full-time consecration can feel like.

This is good news. In addition to formal full-time service, what might happen if we held our marriage partnerships as intentionally as those other realms of dedicated sanctification? In my experience, a continual purification can take place when we wake

---

reason, my partner may fully give themselves to me, completely unguarded."

up to the disturbances we are feeling every day of our intimate relationships. We can go from sacrament meeting repentance, to every few days repentance, to everyday, and eventually moment-to-moment intentionality to wake up to our internal avoidance of our present experience.

In fact, our partner disturbing us can become the spark that brings us back to our highest selves. Bringing our awareness to our immediate, embodied experience of each interaction can become second nature, and there's no better place to practice than with your best/worst trainer: your partner.

When I first started using these practices myself, I was blown away by how many times I had to repeat them. At first, I did what I suggest—take a few key moments and work them out on a sensation level in private. Quickly, I wanted to move to in-the-moment practice. It was intense. Because the practice wasn't smooth yet, I found myself losing track during the conversations or interactions we were having, mostly due to the sensations in my body being so loud. It was strange to feel flooded by opening the lid just a crack, but the flow was intense, perhaps because it had built up some.

I decided to take this stuff pretty seriously, meaning that I wanted to focus on it consistently. I wasn't white-knuckling myself or getting too uptight about it, but I really wanted to see what fruits this practice could bring. I started using more and more moments of my life as opportunities to enter the crucible. My work as a therapist provided many opportunities to practice, and I remember a few sessions in particular where I did the practice (internal 5-10 second rounds) over fifty times in one hour. This was more about me as a person, and my personal historical baggage, than it was about my client's actions or behavior. The people I work with are truly amazing and I really admire each of them. And yet, somehow just *them being them* can really trigger me sometimes.

For many weeks I continued this practice. I still do, actually. It's becoming more and more second nature, and I find myself sometimes even easing my sensation-level tension automatically and effortlessly. It's no surprise, though, that there's one place that keeps on giving me a run for my money: home life. Yes, being in a relationship is consistently the place where I am the most activated, take the longest to recover, and keep finding hidden treasures of internal disturbance. What's more, I don't take disturbance to be any kind of signal regarding the success or failure of me or our partnership—it's simply the nature of being in relationship with humans. It belongs. We can savor it, while also improving if we sense pain and suffering.

I've recently taken to checking in with my conduct as a human the first few hours of the morning, as well as the last few hours of the day. Why? These are the times I'm usually with my wife and three kids, and so the times when I'm most activated and disturbed. Go figure! Again, the crucible of close relationship is a sacred nudge into my immediate, embodied (very loud) experience. Even after thousands of reps at this point, disturbance is ever-present, but I experience it as less and less problematic. Perhaps something in me is beginning to accept the reality of a disturbing life that isn't actually problematic.

One last note here (which could be TMI, so feel free to skip) that has actually been incredibly helpful: my perineum is my compass. I read *Radical Wholeness* by Philip Shepherd and, for some reason, it really impacted me. He works with embodiment as the entry-point into greater being as wholeness, and frequently recommends the perineum or pelvic floor as the resting point. I started using this practice and found that when that area of my body is settled, it's very difficult to fight against sensory experience. Instead, I stay open to what's here, now.

So, in my daily, sacred, messy crucible of an existence, as I have disturbance, the activation in my body triggers some automatic processes:

1) I feel the sensation

2) I try to stay and rest as open (soft pelvic floor, calm mind, centerless awareness)

3) I remain there as the intensity tries to blast me into annihilation

4) I (usually) stay alive

5) Life keeps going

6) I try to act from my highest self

It feels like a thousand tiny scraps of paper are falling off the piñata. All the layers of my habituated shaping, contouring, and pivoting around embodied immediacy are dissolving, and the chances of my old patterns surviving are bleak. In some ways this is good news, because I can love my wife and kids in new and better ways; I can act from new intentions. In some ways, there's a serene sadness that attends some of this work, as the nostalgia, familiarity, and companionship of those childhood patterns fades away into wherever things come from.

It all feels sacred to me, sometimes. Other times, it's just exhausting and intense. And then, being taps me on the shoulder and reminds me that *just this* is already perfect, and there's nothing to fear or pull away from. And it's sacred again—workable, beautiful, just right. Then, my wife looks at me "the wrong way," and we're back into the land of disturbance. And it's okay, and it's disturbing, and something way beyond me still wants to bless the moment with anything that is coming through. The crucible of relationship holds it all, invites it all, purifies it all as Anna and I run into each other over, and over, and over again. Even rough stones can roll.

Let's Check In:

Someone may have a fairly stabilized experience of being backgrounding all of their daily experiences. This means, effectively, that they could sustain any relationship under any relative circumstances. But, should they? Discernment is essential, and just because someone could stay in a certain marriage or partnership doesn't mean they should. Ironically, when someone feels that they actually could sustain a difficult moment, they also feel empowered to finally leave it.

Resting in the ground of being isn't a trick to increase or sustain suffering—it's a gateway to move out of it and fight against it with greater power. When we stabilize our being capacities, we are free to experience any feeling at any time. We're fully free and fully feeling.[11]

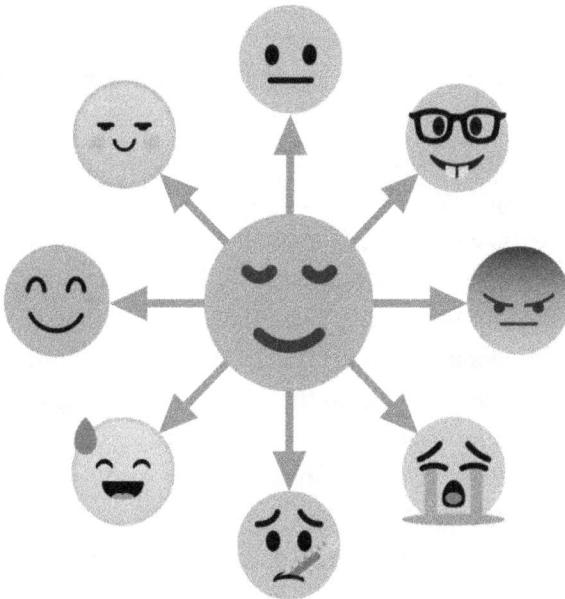

---

11 Dustin DiPerna, personal communication Aug 2024.

THE GOD BLOCK

As I wax a little poetic and share personal reflections on my current relationship with disturbance in partnership, an important note comes up: spiritual bypassing. I mentioned this earlier, noting how we sometimes take a "bigger" spiritual perspective in order to actually avoid intensity, disturbance, and the get-your-hands-dirty work. This is where the Church, or God, can be used to continue our patterns of internal division.

In couples therapy, I had a supervisor and trainer point out something he called the "God Block."[12] It was his term for the pattern that many local Christian couples had of not showing up for their partners because "God's got it." Because they trusted in God's infinite grace and mercy, they could conveniently disengage from their partner and just "pray for them." This could be a strong invitation for the partner to give up the fantasy that their partner was coming to their rescue. In some sense, it can lead to actually facing the disturbing embodiment I'm suggesting. But, from the blocker's side, it seemed to come from a place of checking out, numbing, and leaning out of compassion instead of into it.

When it comes to the LDS Church, we can sometimes check out of our experience via spiritual practice. We might escape to a ward activity, a calling, or scripture study instead of embracing the fullness of our immediate, sensory experience. We might also point a partner to spiritual resources, encouraging them to fix themselves using church practices so that we don't have to deal with their ways of being. In the world of resolving our internal divisions and embracing this moment to its fullest, anything can be a barrier to the work, even something seemingly as holy as temple worship.

Of course, I'm not hoping to make any claims about when, how, or what to do to take care of ourselves. I personally have needed many kinds of spiritual practice to build up a container

---

12 Ryan Rana, The Joshua Center.

to face disturbance, so I do advocate for deliberate work in this realm. But, the energy inside of us, the aliveness we feel in the body, right before we go into these activities seems important. Too often I've found myself and others using spiritual practice as a knee-jerk reaction to internal discomfort. We hear bad news and immediately we pray for the affected. This is good! And, can we sense ourselves in this moment? Is the prayer happening from a heart that is fully feeling or is prayer an attempted escape from the immediate intensity?

When our partner comes to us to resolve a conflict, do we say, "Hey, let's pray together first," because we can't take the intensity of sitting with them? Sometimes we might be falling into needing things to be nice with our partner, and using church teachings, practices, or doctrine to further the bubble-wrap between us and disturbance. We might invite or pressure our partner to engage in church activity because we're not sure how to hold the intensity of just sharing our fears, complaints, and pain with them. By pushing them off into church circles, we may inwardly hope that our partner changes so that they don't disturb us as much.

Sadly, we try to prevent disturbance, when in reality, the gospel path *is* a path of disturbance. If you choose to read and believe the scriptures, you will be disturbed. If you choose to get married, you will have moments of being very disturbed. If you choose to have kids, you win the disturbance lottery. The path of discipleship is a path of living, embodied intensity, and Jesus leads the way, teaching us how to drink bitterness beyond our belief.

When spiritual bypassing, or a God Block, comes into partnership, we accidentally use God in order not to grow up. We use His message to leave His message, and we know not what we do.

Again, try to recall a sense of being whole as we talk about becoming. Feel any sensory experience you're having right now, in your bones and flesh, and consider what's calling out to you, if anything. I personally accept that I block myself from resolving internal divisions and living in embodied immediacy. It happens! And it doesn't change what it is or what it means. I'm not what I could be, yet I'm exactly where I am, and it's just right. See how you can assess yourself with a degree of kindness.

IN- / DEPENDENT WHILE WHOLE

Relationships point out something eternal, as well: We are independent, and we are dependent. They are both completely true. Sometimes leaning into our dependency is our next sacred act, while other times asserting our independence is required.

When it comes to embracing our immediate, embodied experience in its fullness, I don't think I could do it without depending on others. Deep community, physical arms to fall into, and a supportive physical space have been necessary for me to even consider dipping a toe into my disturbance. I can see how dependent I was on those factors in order to explore what it's like to take independent responsibility for my internal experience.

In my opinion, these are normal and healthy cycles of relying on self and relying on others, all held in a greater container. Whether we are hurt in relationship or healed in relationship, or both, my experience has been that relying on community is essential for a new, agentic aliveness to take hold. Internal divisions can resolve when external divisions dissolve, and vice versa.

Disturbance in partnership has helped me feel like a whole person who is in relationship with a whole person, as we roll through life together as both separate and connected beings sharing the same light.[13] Eventually we can come to a space where our sense of inside/outside, self/other, and individuals/community take on new dynamics. These new patterns change the way a partnership, or a group, can be together.

---

13 Shel Silverstein, *The Missing Piece Meets the Big O*.

CHAPTER 6:

DISTURBANCE AS PART OF THE WARD EXPERIENCE

Similar to our solo experience of unconsciously dividing from aspects of ourselves, groups also orphan off people and experiences they cannot tolerate. Groups try to optimize for things like consistency, stability, and identity, and will try to slice away pieces of troubling tissue when they don't know how to handle them.

Latter-day Saint wards are such an interesting place to explore this phenomenon. In this chapter, we'll look at how we, as collectives of Saints, are forced to reckon with ourselves as we engage with each other. We'll explore how a congregation can attack, conform, or numb out to the disturbing parts of itself. And perhaps we can use the collective disturbance in wards to catalyze divine being and becoming. I'll offer some inspiring things I've seen members and leadership do to use the crucible of a collective for the benefit of all.

YOU DON'T PICK YOUR WARD MEMBERS, THANK GOODNESS!

As we saw with codependency in marriage, in a group we can go outward or inward to try and resolve our inner disturbances. When we try the outward approach in a ward, we attempt to control the environment in order to feel better inside. We often find, however, that group dynamics are out of our control and continually bring us disruption. After attempting to control what other church members say, think, feel, and do around us, we begin to realize that we're outnumbered; this approach usually can't be an effective long-term solution to our inner discomfort while in the group. And, since we can't change wards willy-nilly, we are invited to confront collective life again and again.

We can thank God for ward boundaries. It is, perhaps, one of the best ways to bring gospel principles into action. Geographical boundaries aren't without flaw, but in my ward experiences, they've forced me into tight quarters with people I wouldn't usually choose to associate with. Not because I necessarily point my nose up or down at them, although that's probably true to some degree, but because no other part of our lives would bring us under the same roof.

For a few years in my late twenties, I continued going to church despite my internal flame for the faith going out. It was a rote attendance that felt more like drudgery than discipleship. I would spend most of the time worried more about how my little kids were acting than about any spiritual nourishment or service. And, I would often look around the congregation and say to myself, "I don't know if I really want to be any of these people in twenty years."

Honestly, I was really dried up. Burned out. The Church seemed so irrational and brainwashy, and the local members affirmed to me weekly that they were okay with the way it was. Obviously, I was having a hard time finding much value in the organization and practices of the Church. If only I could've hand-picked who was in my congregation and who was in my Sunday School! At the same time that I was feeling rather burned out at church, I was feeling quite alive in my personal study of meditation and human psychology.

Going to church brought me face to face with the truth that I had no idea how to reconcile gospel with science. And this dance of seeming opposites wouldn't let up for me. How nice it would have been to backpedal into reassurance, but the Church doesn't let you transfer wards very easily. (Though the Church is quite helpful when you're moving.)

Despite my earlier conclusions that my congregation was a little stagnant for me, I now believe there's a deep wisdom to the ward experience.[1] Close quarters require us to trust more deeply and move into relationship more intentionally if we want to stay around. We can also learn to differentiate from others once in a while, and at other times we learn to align with collective momentum. Sometimes it was easier for me to go with the flow into or out of the Church. At those times, the more difficult thing was to locate in myself why I was disturbed and how my being and becoming were creating meaning at church.

Herein lies the mess and beauty of the Latter-day Saint ward: we are so close that the sweat, tears, and love we excrete gets all over, and we have to either face it or hide it.

---

1 Dustin DiPerna, *Evolution's Ally: Our World's Religious Traditions as Conveyor Belts of Transformation.*

APPROACHES TO COLLECTIVE DISTURBANCE

"Jesus said to them, 'When you make the two one, and when you make the inside like the outside and the outside like the inside, and the above like the below... then will you enter the kingdom.'"[2]

Ward life, with its beauty and horror, can be seen as an expanded version of the personal, inner life. Previously, we've looked closely at how individuals can resolve their inner divisions through recognizing, tolerating, accepting, loving, and eventually committing completely to all of their experiences. The mind stops shrinking away from anything happening in the heart, mind, and body. This results in a person without inner division, where all experience is met with unconditional kindness—an interior Zion. The seven-stage process of resolving inner divisions implies that there are different parts inside of us that push, pull, reject, or accept one another. The individual's mission is to find a deep ground from which to hold all experience and then to practice relating to intensity with greater and greater trust, kindness, and acceptance.

When we expand this process from the individual to the collective (in this case a Latter-day Saint ward), the same patterns and principles apply. Instead of parts of ourselves relating to other inner parts, though, there are a few hundred individuals relating to each other. Ward members have options: they can attack one another, avoid, ignore, shrink, tolerate, accept, embrace, expand, or commit completely to each other's lived experiences.

Before diving in, I want to be clear that many people have experienced very real challenge, pain, and trauma in Latter-day Saint settings. For many, a healthy and appropriate choice is to create space and boundaries, including leaving the Church. Doing so is not necessarily a sign of weakness, low willpower,

---

2 Gospel of Thomas, Saying 22.

avoidance, or sin, in my experience. For this section, I want to explore how those that choose to stay in the Church might deal with disturbance.

Since I've counseled many Latter-day Saints around the hurt and trauma that congregation living has brought, I'd like to take some space here to reflect how collective dynamics can sometimes bring us real pain and disturbance. Not all wards operate this way, but many do.

Most wards I have been in, and most wards described by my clients, deal with disturbance and intensity in much the same way—they invite conformity. Perhaps this is related to the gravitational momentum of the Church on the development scales,[3] but the trend I see is that men who conform to authority and are very actively doing and becoming what they're supposed to, tend to be asked to fill leadership positions (elders quorum president, bishop, stake leadership, etc.). Rarely do I see the guy wearing the blue shirt in sacrament meeting invited to take a position of leadership. Instead, it's usually the well-groomed white shirt who is called to authority—it's the one who has external signs of aligning with Church practices and customs.

The reason this may be important is that it begins to shape how the collective body of a ward deals with deviation, a seemingly significant cause of disturbance in ward settings. Someone, or some group of someones, will begin to show covert or overt signs of deviating from the (sometimes unspoken) agreed-upon norms. It could be what people are wearing, or the language they use, or more direct approaches like speaking out or writing to leadership. Oftentimes, these invitations to explore something just beyond the comfort of the group are like the kettle whistling on the stove—something is moving and grooving and needs to be heard and released.

---

3 See McConkie's *Navigating Mormon Faith Crisis: A Simple Developmental Map* for a deeper dive into how stages of growth can help us understand how and why Saints differ in their understanding and practice of the Faith.

But, because many of our wards aren't sure what to do with deviation, it is often met with a kind of aggression. Usually not physical aggression or even verbal aggression, but an aggression in the sense that responses from leadership and ward members are usually cordial on the surface, but saturated in aversion, tension, or passive unacceptance. Going back to our Seven Stages of Dissolving Internal Divisions, the very first step is the recognition that *we are divided*, and that it's costing us big time. I haven't personally been in many wards that openly recognize the fact that we have strategies in place to tamp down deviation, vulnerabilities, and our bleeding, lively edges, but it might look like this: let's say Shelby isn't satisfied with the way women are represented in sacrament meetings. She may feel that there's a heavy visible presence of men up front: three bishopric members, a dozen young men, a speaker or two, a visiting stake leader, and sometimes the organist or chorister. *Dang, that's like a 15 to 1 ratio*, she thinks.

To align, Shelby may stay quiet, blocking out internal feelings of dissonance or unease. She could open inwardly to these sensations and meet them with kindness, finding that she can be whole while having these sensations. Then, she might ask how to genuinely improve the situation. If she wants to deviate, how could she bring this forward? How could she bring to light, for the benefit of herself and the group, the fact that some members feel unsettled about how things go on during church?

Can she get up to the pulpit and voice it in front of everyone? Take a second. Imagine a woman getting up during a Fast and Testimony meeting and pointing to the disturbance she feels, and perhaps others feel, regarding this male-lopsided physical display on the stand.

How do you, dear reader, feel in your body right now as you read that? Open or closed? Loose or tight? Settled or bracing? Just notice how you individually feel, and then imagine the aroma in the chapel that might waft in as she speaks her experiential truth. What is the collective reaction to a deviating message?

Having made it this far in the book, you may have noticed how bracing and dividing from the immediate reality of our moments has its gifts (surviving as youngsters) but also has severe limitations as adults (we organize life around avoiding disturbance instead of around our highest, divine intentions). This is no different on a group level, in my opinion.

After Shelby sits down from sharing the truth of her immediate experience, what's the aftertaste in the room? And, how would others in the crowd know if they're allowed to say:

"YES, thank you so much for that" or

"Gosh, she's really struggling..."

My experience is that many members are looking *toward leadership* to know what to feel about what's going on. In general, our group of Saints isn't very differentiated. (Differentiation is when we're able to feel internally settled enough to hold personal experience intact while staying open to differing external experiences. It's the inner thermometer for how much difference we can stay open and engaged with.) So, *they look outside* to see if they're *allowed to feel something on the inside*. It's a normal response early in life, and it serves us quite well then. Think about it—a three-yr-old comes across a new creature (an opossum) while on a local trail hike with mommy. He can't quite tell how he should feel about it, so he looks up to mommy's face. If she cowers in fear, so does he, and they book it to safety. If her face softens in delight and wonder, he can soften too, All is Well!

We learn about the world from an outside compass (our caregivers) before our inner compass develops. In general, this keeps humans around longer because lessons of life can be transferred without the pain and harm the previous humans paid to learn the lesson. Eventually, though, we need to learn to use our own inner compass, our own light to illuminate our path. As we all know, oil in our *own lamp* is really what counts when the big party starts.

Let's get back to sacrament meeting. Shelby sits down, there's some tension, and people are looking for an answer. Is she off her rocker or onto something here, people? For many Saints right now, there's only one thing that can begin to soothe their neck tension: the stamp of approval from authority. Suggestions for deviation from the bottom up are usually met with a kind of bracing and avoidance, but as soon as a letter comes from authority (this is the new "what's mommy's face doing?"), All is Well.

I've seen this several times, where someone will voice something contrary to current practices and be met with an attack, an invitation to quiet down, or with the blank stare of being simply ignored. They're rarely celebrated. Then, a few weeks, months, or years later, a message from the proper authority arrives bearing the same message that the contrarian delivered. Only this time, the group response is so different: "Finally, the Restoration continues its unfolding! Black members can have the Priesthood, women can wear pants, teens aren't told not to "neck" each other, we're allowed to talk about Joseph's wives now!" And it's true—things are always unfolding, always new.

The new message from authority matches the contrarian's, but who bears it becomes what's most important. This mode of learning truth—top-down revelation—has its place. Yet, I'm curious to see what happens when the circle we draw around authority for revelation grows to include more and more of the body of Christ. Of course, either way can certainly go too far. Regardless of the details, the pattern of looking to the head of the congregation is usually how I see wards currently deal with disturbance. Requests surrounding a deviation are sometimes met with leadership responses like these:

"I'll have to consult the manual."

"I'll have to talk to the Stake President about that one."

"Let me ponder and pray on this to see what God really wants here."

I've wondered lately what happens when leadership responds, instead, with one of these:

> "Wow, I can feel that you're pointing to an important gap in our current experience, and I want to say yes to moving into a potentially disturbing confrontation with you."

> "Every experience of each of our members is a part of us. I feel some personal difficulty here, *and* this conversation fully belongs here—thank you for bringing it."

> "My heart cannot help but be completely open to everything you're saying right now, and I feel like you're speaking for many of us. I'm committed to embracing what you're bringing and needing at this moment in our ward."

Sister Runia helped burst our avoidance bubble in General Conference when she invited us to respond from a deeper well of compassion, sometimes beyond our normal range of comfort:

> *"Our family feels whole and complete because you are in it." "You will be loved for the rest of your life—no matter what."*

> *Sometimes what we need is empathy more than advice; listening more than a lecture; someone who hears and wonders, "How would I have to feel to say what they just said?"*[4]

I'm delighted to hear more and more stories that show me that leadership and the collective momentum of Saints leans into a wider embrace of the ward members' experiences.

With an intention to have our Zion of one heart and one mind, can we truly arrive there without bringing more voices to the table? Can we, in sacrament meeting and Sunday school, "regardless of whether we like or dislike what arises in our [group] experience... *become* most reliably the *activity of kindness*"?[5] There are many paths to conformity, including aggression and ignoring, but I believe there is only one path to having one heart and one mind.

---

4 Tamara W. Runia, "Seeing God's Family through the Overview Lens."

5 Bruce Tift, *Already Free*, 54.

For me, it is the fundamental sensibility of a full-hearted, personal commitment to embrace every internal sensory experience, unguarded, as a mother holds her infant, a hen gathers her chicks, or the Savior kisses His Mother's cheek.

BEING AND BECOMING AS A WARD

Wards that struggle with disturbances in the group can benefit from looking at where they fall on the being and becoming scale. A ward that is lopsided on the being side will most likely have lots of good vibes and may not know how to act to improve the real-life circumstances that surround them. A congregation that is lopsided on becoming may be doing so much to improve, change, and develop that it cannot feel the moment-to-moment peace of God that permeates every moment, regardless of how much striving and driving we do.

As we've seen in previous chapters, being and becoming each have an essential role in the grand experience of mortality. Our previously mentioned two-step authentication can be helpful here:

1) Fully embrace and accept the moment in all of its truth
2) From this place of acceptance, genuinely wonder how to improve the situation

This is my ward, in all its beauty and mess, and I accept every piece of it. I don't pull away internally, even a micro-muscle's amount, from the truth of what's here. All of it belongs right now, and I say Yes to it.

From this Yes, and not out of a need for anything to happen, how can we improve this ward? How can this moment, this situation, our group of humans act in ways that align with our deepest intentions? What light-filled future is trying to peek through? Let's act now.

From a ward perspective, this way of relating to the congregation doesn't come from one individual. It emerges out of the many parts of the collective like a pot of stew. Often, you may notice that Sunday school lessons and testimony meetings have a rhythm to them. A theme will kick up, then get emphasized, then be adjusted slightly with added nuance, and then hop categories while still sharing the same essence.

Intentionally or not, humans have a way of syncing up, of entraining one to the other, to create a whole that is larger than the sum of the parts. I've seen a skilled, wholeness-oriented Saint ask a six-second question that completely shifted the next forty-five minutes of elders quorum. Several members of my local ward have an ability to testify from such a raw, trusting place that my heart just falls open to my own rawness and trust and the next thing I know I'm operating from that place as well.

A new "entity" emerges in these moments. It's not quite a *thing*, but it's also *not a nothing*. The room is filled with a savoring quality that the body's and heart's taste buds are especially sensitive to. A blanket of greater sanctification begins to fall from the sky, and minds and hearts begin unifying. Something beyond the moment seeks to be known, something beautiful, good, and whole.

Like a skittish animal, though, it can be scared off by human tension and fear. When collective momentum moves away from acceptance and kindness of each expression, the field can break, and our smaller, separate selves can again get lost in unhealthy being or becoming.

Contracting back into our conditioned, reactive selves is not a problem from a context of wholeness. But when we lose the backdrop of wholeness *and* revert to reactivity, we can break the collective field that is midwifing us into a greater union. Even though we may not be able to articulate it in the moment, our soft animal bodies can sense when the collective presence wants us either to conform to its experiential threshold or to wake up to our continual wholeness and potential. A collective ward field, grounded in wholeness by leaders and members, can invite us back to a home we already inhabit, again and again.

Let's Check In:

We've seen how an individual can hold the ground of being as a backdrop to everything in us that is disturbed, delighted, and transformed. On a collective level, the same dynamics exist, but this time there are many individuals casting votes on what to background or foreground. Many vie for their individual preference: being, becoming, or both. The beautiful thing about collective life is that it's made of individuals just like you. Simply by holding an inner sensibility and adding your voice (or silence) to the moment, you can point the entire group to a new way to meet this collective moment. The individual is always steering the group, and the group the individual.

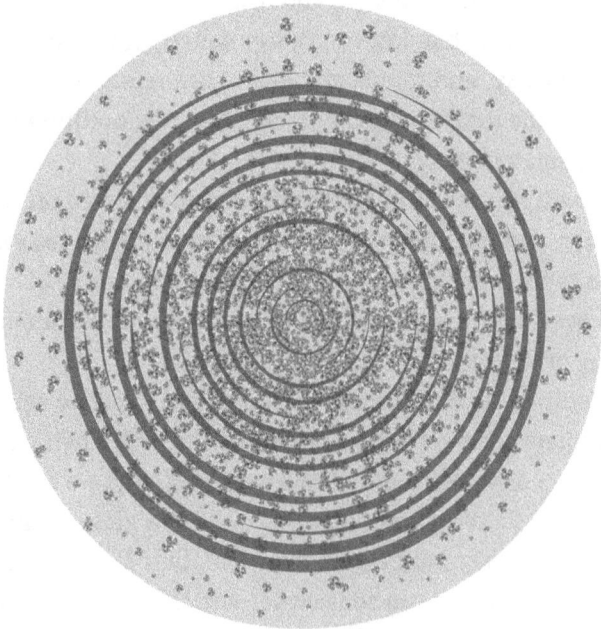

THE ILLUSION OF SEPARATENESS

As much as our immediate experience can hint to us that we're separate beings arriving in separate cars and living in separate houses, there's a greater reality before us that invites us to sense our complete interdependence. We aren't separate beings; we are interbeings.[6]

On a physical level, our inhale is the exhale of a tree. Our digestion is the work of thousands of microbes and living organisms. Our commute to work is the work of construction workers, car engineers, oil harvesters and refiners, and a complex electric grid. I can say "I drove to work today" and that's true, and it's also true that the driving required and depended upon thousands of others being as they are, so I can be as I am. Interbeing.

When we eat an apple, where do we start and stop? Before I eat the apple, I may say I'm not the apple. Then after I eat it, it becomes me. I digest it. Its nutrients and carbohydrates power my body and mind. The physical matter of that apple will translate into muscle movement, cell regrowth, and brain activity. The apple is now part of my mental thought activity, it's part of my job, it's part of my ability to write this sentence, and it's part of my bathroom experience a day or two later.

Am I the apple? Yes and no. And where did the apple start and stop? Who delivered it, washed it, picked it, watered it, trimmed the tree, or planted the tree? Where did that water come from, how did those particles of H_2O evaporate into the sky and return as rain, and how did the sun find its place in our system? As you can see, if we keep going, we find that it's hard to find anything about us that is just us. We've done this exercise physically, but it extends from there into all of mental, emotional, and spiritual life as well. We aren't just human beings, we're human interbeings.

A wonderful modern-day seer, Thich Nhat Hanh, has commented on this reality in his poem "Please Call Me by My True

---

6 Thich Nhat Hanh, *Interbeing: Fourteen Guidelines for Engaged Buddhism.*

Names." In it, he shows how he has many names as he embraces the reality of his interbeing.

Please Call Me by My True Names – Thich Nhat Hanh

Don't say that I will depart tomorrow —
even today I am still arriving.

Look deeply: every second I am arriving
to be a bud on a Spring branch,
to be a tiny bird, with still-fragile wings,
learning to sing in my new nest,
to be a caterpillar in the heart of a flower,
to be a jewel hiding itself in a stone.

I still arrive, in order to laugh and to cry,
to fear and to hope.

The rhythm of my heart is the birth and death
of all that is alive.

I am the mayfly metamorphosing
on the surface of the river.
And I am the bird
that swoops down to swallow the mayfly.

I am the frog swimming happily
in the clear water of a pond.
And I am the grass-snake
that silently feeds itself on the frog.

I am the child in Uganda, all skin and bones,
my legs as thin as bamboo sticks.
And I am the arms merchant,
selling deadly weapons to Uganda.

I am the twelve-year-old girl,
refugee on a small boat,
who throws herself into the ocean
after being raped by a sea pirate.

And I am the pirate,
my heart not yet capable
of seeing and loving.

I am a member of the politburo,
with plenty of power in my hands.
And I am the man who has to pay
his "debt of blood" to my people
dying slowly in a forced-labor camp.

My joy is like Spring, so warm
it makes flowers bloom all over the Earth.
My pain is like a river of tears,
so vast it fills the four oceans.

Please call me by my true names,
so I can hear all my cries and my laughter at once,
so I can see that my joy and pain are one.

Please call me by my true names,
so I can wake up,
and so the door of my heart
can be left open,
the door of compassion.

To really allow a flourishing of our wards, we have to come to the reality of our interbeing. I am:

- the conservative LDS man whose testimony never varies from "I know _____ to be true."
- the excommunicated bishop who cheated on his wife.
- the prophet of God, spokesman of Divinity, and his ministry and message.
- the ashamed teenager who cannot share at church what has happened to them or who they take themselves to be.
- the toddler eating cereal in the pew.
- the beaming missionary whose light radiates in a busy, crowded street.

Just as we can dissolve internal divisions individually, we can dissolve our collective internal ward divisions as we share in a heartfelt communion and generosity of Spirit. What is the natural state of a ward when it stops clenching? What kind of rest, warmth, and presence can fill the space when we splay ourselves out, fully unguarded to the reality of who we are? When the scales of division fall from our eyes, we might see,

> *"the secret beauty of [our] hearts, the depths of [our] hearts where neither sin nor desire nor self-knowledge can reach, the core of [our] reality, the person that each one is in God's eyes. If only [we] could all see [our]selves as we really are. If only we could see each other that way all the time. There would be no more war, no more hatred, no more cruelty, no more greed. . . But this cannot be seen, only believed and 'understood' by a peculiar gift."[7]*

From this place of deep accepting, or even savoring the truth of our congregational experience, we can ask ourselves what is to be done. How can I hold myself? Or hold my neighbor? My leader, teacher, and student?

We become one heart and one mind not because we're replicas of each other, but because there are no divisions between us. All are supported in their fullness. And when no barriers exist, Zion is one.

LATTER-DAY SAINT WHILE WHOLE

I won't pretend to have all the answers here, just field notes. And, I want to be generous in sharing what unique perspective and vision I have.

I truly believe that our emerging wholeness as a Latter-day Saint community is a complete mystery. It will surprise me, delight me, disappoint me, and perhaps be just what I need.

---

7 Thomas Merton, *Conjectures of a Guilty Bystander.*

And, in that spirit, here are a few hopes and dreams that come to me as I envision a future that starts from whole and keeps getting better:

WHOLE MEMBERS

Members who hold the view of their wholeness continually can flow through a congregation with grace and vulnerability. They can be radically available to comfort others, or to be comforted. They can rest deeply, quietly, and engage silently from their heart, or they can stand up and speak more directly from love than we're used to.

Whole members can lead out or follow in. They can show up or disappear and they know that whatever they're offering to the group, it is enough. They sense in their bones that as they follow their inner compass, it will also be the best for the group. They know they are individuals and they know they are the group.

These members forgive quickly. They intend to stay unguarded from their faults or from the revelation of the impact of their faults. They also aren't afraid of their strengths or their light. They deeply engage or disengage in life, as needed, and are full of love.[8]

WHOLE LEADERS

Whole leaders resolve their internal divisions and therefore don't attempt to divide or hide themselves from others' experiences. They don't shy away from certain meetings, and they also don't shy away from canceling or reducing meetings that aren't needed, even if it's traditional to hold them. They know that preserving the integrity of gospel teachings with exactness is paramount, but

---

8 John Kesler, *Integral Polarity Practice in Service of Leadership for Flourishing.*

they also live the spirit of the Law and can "damn the policy!" when teachings get in the way of embracing a disturbed member.

Whole leaders are sensitive to their becoming and know that they have blind spots. They can acknowledge how limited their understanding is, but they can also boldly stand in their truth and stop pretending they don't know what they truly know in their bones.

Whole leaders don't need to be seen, but they are fine being seen when it's appropriate. They can serve endlessly and also cancel their day and rest when that's what's needed. They are humble and they are also proud—radiant.

Leaders of our wards are men and women. They are certainly children and infants, because whole leaders realize they are also students, and students are their teachers. Whole leaders can need nothing and need everything to be what they need to be.

WARDS OF WHOLENESS

Wards of wholeness have a deep structure that allows all experience to be embraced as it is and improved. They are also so flexible and amorphous that they can be anything they need to be, within their very real limitations. These wards have official boundaries, lists of members, and schedules, but everyone knows that everyone is trying to be here for the right reasons, and all the institutional stuff is there to support them, not the other way around.

These wards can sense when they are tilting into too much of a good thing—be it being or becoming. They are okay with the lowliest of members or the loftiest of leaders pointing it out, and all hope to be responsive to one another. Wards of wholeness realize they are made of little parts called individuals, but they also realize that no individual exists without the whole.

Wards of wholeness can be incubators for Divinity.

CONCLUSION:

ENTERING THE REST OF THE LORD NOW, REGARDLESS OF CIRCUMSTANCE

What are we waiting for?

Or, in case that question brings up an idea that we're not already here, can you taste the rest of the Lord right now? I don't mean that generally, as in, can you taste it this year? As you read or hear these words, are you already here, resting in His goodness and wholeness?

It's my experience that we can begin tasting what it's like to put on the mind and heart of Christ. Many of us have had that experience, radiating a love beyond our capacities, saying words we've never conceived, and acting with a power we didn't know could come through us. And then, a few hours later, we might snap at our kids. The mind of Christ leaves us! Or, maybe it feels like we're leaving it. Maybe our "leaving" is just preparing for more of it, a natural cycle of ebb and flow.

What happens when it stops leaving—when our dominant state shifts to the mind of Christ, continually? I've seen the effects of a human unfolding their Divinity in small doses and then stabilizing it until it pervades every aspect of their lives. My spine tingles just remembering these people. Their liveliness is a little scary, honestly, like there's too much light coming out of their eyes. They almost seem out of this world, because they are. And aren't. They're living fully in a mortal and divine realm at the same time, witnessing the radiant love of God's light manifesting in the world around them, continually. Life is complete, always, sealed as God's forever, and getting better all the time.

May we become perfected from our deepest place of perfect being.

APPENDIX I: GOSPEL JAZZ FESTIVAL

Tasting a wholeness, for me, invites regenerative collaboration. Here are a few gospel-related improvs that use a set of chord progressions and cadences you're used to, but might have a new line or two to inspire you in your own compositional movements.

My experience is that I can't really tell how the song of wholeness will show its face in our lives. My singular perspective is just one, and I'm intrigued at how others see wholeness joining them in life. So, I've asked a few folks in these spheres to chime in. Let the music begin.

PARENTING FROM WHOLENESS

– *Haymitch St. Stephen*

Adam fell that men might be; and men are, that they might have joy.

This is, perhaps, one of the most well known scriptures from *The Book of Mormon*. And why shouldn't it be? Situating joy as the fundamental aim of humanity sounds great. After all, who doesn't want more joy in their life? But I find the context of this passage to be interesting. Lehi is teaching his kids some beautiful truths, albeit in the form of a lengthy lecture. It feels like Lehi has sat his family down for early morning scripture study and he is going to savor every minute of his precious monologue before his suffering children can finally exclaim, "Dad, we're gonna be late for school!" While I love the philosophical and spiritual ground on which Lehi is standing, I can't help but wonder if Latter-day Saint parents too often share Lehi's good intentions, while mimicking his painfully un-joyful delivery. So what might a more joyful parenting posture look like?

For the sake of offering a wildly different approach to parenting, I want to paint a picture of the family culture I come from. It might seem indulgent, hedonistic, or downright offensive to some. But my intention is to share with you how my parents' approach ultimately prioritized gospel joy over all else. They were not, nor are they today, perfect parents. Rather they are saints, striving toward King Benjamin's definition of the word: submissive, meek, humble, patient, full of love, and willing to submit to all things which the Lord seeth fit to inflict upon them. My parents' joy put off the natural man and cultivated a home of wholeness where I felt that I lacked nothing and could become whatever I dreamed. Let me tell you some stories.

My parents are submissive. I remember being in third grade when a big snowstorm hit town. Living on the mountain, deep snow was not the kind of thing that canceled plans. But that day, my mom asked me if I wanted to stay home and play in the new snow instead of going to school. So I stayed, and I played. And she played with me. We even convinced the neighbors to stay home and play with us. And though I was embarrassed by my teacher the next day in front of class, I knew my mom wasn't going to let school get in the way of my real education. She taught me to submit to the joy of the unexpected.

My parents are meek. My dad was a ski rep his entire career. In a ski town, that equates to being a bit of a local legend. One day, several teenagers from the neighborhood came by looking for some swag. My dad's ski company had partnered with one of the new energy drink companies, but nobody in our family really took a liking to the beverages. So my dad gladly unloaded several cases on these kids, who were over-the-moon at their luck. It didn't take long before my dad received a phone call from one of the kids' mothers, "Bishop, I just caught my son with a bag full of energy drinks and he had the audacity to say you gave them to him!" My dad gently assured this sister that he had, and that he trusted her son. He taught me meekness through his demeanor, more so than any words could have ever conveyed.

My parents are humble. They helped me pay my way through college. I remember telling them about Road to the Shire—what ultimately became the capstone project for my degree. It was clear they didn't understand what the project was about, how it fulfilled my course requirements, or if it would even enable me to graduate (to be fair, very few people understood it at the time, including most of my professors). What my parents did understand, when I told them I was missing two weeks of class during my senior year to go to New Zealand dressed as a hobbit, was that this project brought me joy. That seemed to be all they really needed to know in order to offer their full support. To me, that demonstrated huge humility in their willingness to defer to my judgment and joy rather than assert their knowingness, even though they were paying for my tuition.

My parents are patient. I don't know if many parents imagine their son will still be living with them at age 35. And though I have moved out several times, I am once again living with them at the time of this writing. As a conceptual artist, I don't have what many might call a "real job." I have two broken cars in their garage (well one, I fixed the other yesterday). I don't have a girlfriend, a 401K, or a salary. They have listened patiently as I have told them about my plans to build an art studio, my use of psychedelic plant medicines, and my dreams to buy an old church. And still they insist on supporting me however they can. My mom is the first person I talk to whenever I have a crazy new idea. And my dad is always reminding me, "Life's rough, then you die." They have helped me raise money for art installations, search for vacant land, and are often telling me that I can live with them as long as I want to. Life hasn't worked out how I thought it would, and I thank God for that because I get to hang out with my parents more because of it.

My parents are full of love. When I was growing up, my best friend was experiencing conflict at home. He had packed up a bag and left, but he only made it as far as our house before my parents took him in. Although the conflict he experienced at home was centered around him breaking rules and sneaking out, my mom and dad gave him a bedroom that had its own entrance/exit. They told him he was free to come and go as he pleased. I heard him leave a lot at night, and I heard his girlfriend in the next room a lot, too. After only a few weeks, he returned to his home and repaired things with his parents. Later in life he told me how significant it was to him that we just loved him unconditionally. Over the years, my parents have let many such drifters stay with us.

My parents are willing to submit to all things which the Lord seeth fit to inflict upon them. Though there is certainly a perspective from which our privileged life as a family has been relatively easy, things for my parents have gotten harder in recent years. My dad, on a church assignment with the young men, crashed his mountain bike a few years ago, losing an eyeball and suffering an intense brain injury. It was like he aged 10 years overnight. He experiences intense memory loss, fatigue, and depression as a result of the accident and old age. His dependence on my mom has increased dramatically, which makes her life incalculably more complex. Handling taxes, medical bills, and credit card statements is hard enough with her ADHD. But she rarely complains. My parents are simply more interested in the joys of life.

I am not a parent so I have no idea how hard parenting actually is. All I hope to do here is pass on the gift my parents have given me, which is something like wholeness. I don't know how or when it happened, but my parents pointed me to my true self. They have shown me how to drink deeply from the abundant cup of life, lacking nothing.

WHOLENESS, IN CONSIDERATION OF THE SECOND COMING

– Lisa Anderson

Every time I park my car in the garage, I come eye-to-eye with four rows of #10 cans on a shelf, neatly labeled for flour, rice, pasta, and oats. These cans have been untouched for years, and will probably keep gathering dust for decades to come. Occasionally I stare at them, but rarely do I think about why they are there.

Here are a few reasons that may, or may not, have brought about the existence of my modest stockpile:

1) A little voice from my past warning that terrible things could happen any day, and that the prophet has told us to be prepared, so if we're not prepared, it's kinda our own fault.

2) Simply wanting to be/feel obedient to prophetic guidance.

3) Ticking a box.

4) The cans look nice on the shelf and make me feel like I've done something proactive by purchasing them.

5) Peace of mind knowing that if we have another pandemic and I really want to bake bread during lock-down, I have a backup stash of flour.

Honestly I think they're all valid reasons, and maybe someday I'll dig further into those motivations. But there is another reason,[1] and it's one that I have a harder time thinking about: preparing for the Second Coming.

For many years, I associated the time of the Second Coming with horror: "the great and dreadful day";[2] "and in that day shall be heard of wars and rumors of wars, and the whole earth shall be in commotion";[3] "and surely, men's hearts shall fail them; for fear shall come upon all people."[4] This was usually accompanied by the proverb, "If ye are prepared ye shall not fear."[5]

On the flipside of this coin, I hear many people speak of the Second Coming with desperate eagerness; it provides hope for an instantaneous (and imminent) end to all trouble and suffering, as expressed in these phrases,

Great is the darkness that covers the earth,

---

1 For a witty summary of the logic behind LDS food storage, check out Eric Widdison's Quora post, "Why do Mormons store food?"

2 Malachi 4:5

3 D&C 45:26

4 D&C 88:91

5 D&C 38:30

Oppression, injustice and pain...
Come, Lord Jesus, come, Lord Jesus...
When out of the heavens You come.
Darkness will vanish, all sorrow will end.[6]

My journey to wholeness is realizing that I don't want to be motivated by fear of darkness, fear of messing up, or fear of being caught unprepared. Instead, I want to be motivated by love and learning and becoming. Likewise, I don't want to put so much expectation into a future deliverance that I neglect to work toward solutions and healing right now.

At the same time, I need to respect those who see the Second Coming through a different lens, including those who feel panic or desperation. Their motivations are significant, and part of their individual journeys. All people, in their own ways, can bring about goodness through their efforts to prepare the earth for His coming.[7] And we cannot underestimate the value and power of hope, for those who truly suffer in this life. I may never have more than four rows of cans on my garage shelf. And I may never exclaim "The end is near!" out of fear, or even out of hope. But I can learn from others how to be more intentional in my choices and thoughts about the future.

While the Second Coming of Christ is in the big picture, I find wholeness by seeking the face of the Lord—His light, love, help, and healing—in the present circumstances. Every day is an opportunity to welcome Him back into my life. I love this phrase from the *Book of Mormon*: "Look forward unto the Messiah, and believe in him to come as though he already was."[8]

---

6 "Come Lord Jesus (Great is the darkness)" by Noel Richards and Faye Simpson.

7 "Preparing for the Lord's Return" by Elder D. Todd Christofferson.

8 Jarom 1:11

FAITH FROM WHOLENESS

—Jon Ogden

Faith from wholeness trusts that everything belongs—the pleasant and the unpleasant, the joy and the sorrow.

It's an insight that surfaces in cultures across the world. The Aztecs worshiped the Deity of Dirt. Hindus worship Kali, goddess of creation and destruction. The Buddhist monk Thich Nhat Hanh says that you can't enjoy the beauty of the lotus without the mud it grows from. "It must needs be that there is an opposition in all things," Lehi says in the *Book of Mormon*. "Wherefore, all things must needs be a compound in one."

Faith from wholeness trusts all of it. It trusts that uncomfortable days or weeks or years are sometimes part of growth. In practice, this looks like surrendering to what is and having faith that we can trust the present. Wisdom traditions around the world speak to this as well, whether they call it acceptance (Buddhism), flowing with the Way (Taoism), letting go of what's beyond your control (Stoicism), taking shelter in the divine (Hinduism), submission (Islam), or "not my will but thine be done" (Christianity).

Surrendering to the present is the only way to experience it. When we don't have faith, we end up saying "not this" to every experience that isn't pleasant. We don't want to do the dishes or sit through a difficult conversation or serve someone who is hard to serve, and so we say, "not this," "not this," and "not this" without realizing that this repetition is training us to say "not this" to all situations — even situations we actually do want.

Faith, by contrast, is saying yes to *this*, whatever *this* is. It's how we align with life itself—how we reach the divine. As the priest and writer Richard Rohr says, "The way to any universal idea is to proceed through a concrete encounter. The one is the way to the many; the specific is the way to the spacious; the now is the way to the always; the here is the way to the everywhere; the material is the way to the spiritual; the visible is the way to the invisible."

In this way, faith is distinct from belief. A Latter-day Saint might believe one thing, a Hindu might believe another, and a Muslim might believe another still. But each one, regardless of belief or disbelief, can access faith from a place of wholeness.

Faith trusts that it all belongs. Faith is when we have *confidence* (a word that literally means "with faith") in the current of life.

APPENDIX II: GAMES AND PLAY

Being and Becoming are sacred. They are also playful and light.

I've found a few fun ways to test out whether or not I'm coming from a place of wholeness. It can be nice to have a litmus test for these kinds of things. If you know you have a shame trigger around not being good enough or being evaluated, skip this section for now. It won't be necessary or helpful yet. If you can hold yourself lightly, check out these games. Remember, you are whole at every stage.

In Western lucid dream training, there's a practice of doing a "state check," which is a simple action that can tell us if we're waking or dreaming.[9] (Kind of like the totems the characters in *Inception* use to see if it's a dream world, only I prefer not to wait twenty-five seconds for my top to stop spinning.)

A basic "state check" in dream training is simply to jump up and down. It's recommended to practice jumping up and down several times a day so that it feels like a normal, even unconscious or automatic part of our being. That way, when we are in a dream, we might just jump up, because it's "what we do." In a waking state, we return to earth at normal gravity. In dreaming, we often float away slightly, or fall too fast, or land

---

9 Andrew Holecek, *Dream Yoga: Illuminating Your Life Through Lucid Dreaming and the Tibetan Yogas of Sleep.*

and sink up to our ankles in the earth, etc. So a simple jump can tell us immediately if we're waking or dreaming.

In that spirit, let's explore some "state checks" to see if we're coming from wholeness or if we've collapsed into our limiting narratives. Monitoring the place from which we start (wholeness, fear, incompleteness, etc.) is a useful skill in stabilizing positive changes we experience in our journey of unveiling our innate goodness. Included are some fun training games and questions that I've used to check or extend my threshold for sustaining wholeness in different settings.

QUESTIONS TO CHECK WHOLENESS

- If I needed to stop my current activity immediately, at any moment, could I?

- If I needed to start any new activity immediately, at any moment, could I?

- Can I feel my feet?[10]

- Is there any part of my experience right now that I feel doesn't belong?

- How is this moment also part of my waking up to my wholeness?

- How is this person's behavior a way their wholeness is trying to reveal itself?

- Can I look at any part of my life and fully accept it? Can I then ask, "How can this change for the better?" Can I stay open, unguarded, and curious?

- When I'm not "getting it right," I feel not enough, or like I'm failing, can I also sense a part of me that is not tarnished? The field of being that is never stained?

---

10 Thanks to Thomas McConkie for the simple and inspiring reminder.

GAMES TO TRAIN, EXPAND, AND CELEBRATE DAILY WHOLENESS[11]

· Coin Flip

Carry a coin in your pocket, or get a phone app that flips coins. At random times throughout the day, pause just before doing a task. Flip the coin and decide which side is a Yes and which side is a No. Follow the coin's decision on whether or not to do the activity.

Great tasks to try this on are common coping mechanisms or distractions, as well as conveniences: Getting a second helping at mealtime. Checking email. Hopping on social media. Booting up a video game. Peeling an orange. Cueing up a podcast or news article. Making love with a partner. Etc. (The ones where you really don't want to do the coin flip are the best ones to practice.)

· Sensing the Opposite

In ordinary moments, see if you can feel the opposite side of the present polarity. If you're at a rock concert, see if you can sense the silence and stillness as well. During physical activity, sense the rest. During conflict, sense the peace. During creativity, sense destruction.

Find moments where you cannot access both sides and practice outside the moment. Then get back into that same moment and try again. Rinse and repeat.

---

11 Note that most of these are in the gross and subtle realm of experience, but in my experience, they've scaled nicely into training awareness.

· Cold Water Plunge or Shower

Experiencing cold water is one of the best practices I've found to embrace disturbance. In this case,
we practice meeting spontaneous and reactionary
physiological contraction with softness.

You might not have consistent access to a body of
cold water, so perhaps begin by slowly turning the
water to cold during a shower. As soon as you feel a
bracing in your body, pause there and breathe until
you soften again. Keep repeating, colder and colder,
until you cannot soften against the cold. Go back to
where you can soften, and end the practice session
for that day.

Keep practicing daily until pure cold elicits no
contraction or bracing in your somatic experience.

Releasing physical contraction under disturbance
is ideal training for more subtle clenching against
sensations, emotions, thoughts, daydreams, urges,
etc. Eventually this same skill of staying open
under duress becomes a key skill in letting ourselves die, both in an egoic birth/death as well as a
physical death.

· Just Do Nothing

Set aside some time just to do nothing. Sit in a
chair and look out the window.

Pause randomly throughout the day and do
nothing for a bit. See if some part of you feels like
the moment got better or worse. This can be very
revealing of how much we are habituated to doing or
becoming as an identity of self.

Doing nothing allows us to sense how much we rely on preoccupation, distraction, and busyness. And we can find out that we're just as wonderful doing nothing, sometimes, as we are doing something.

If you're a meditator, "doing meditation" won't count for this exercise, although you may have gotten into phases of non-meditations that can fit here.

Oftentimes, the best time to do nothing is right before a really important task or overbooked day. Starting by not doing any of it, and feeling complete, is a real check-mate on life's Strive 'n Drive momentum.

· Eye Floaters

One fun way to play with perspectives is to use those eye floaters you can see when you close your eyes. Just try it. Sometimes it helps to look at something bright to see them better. Just hold your gaze with your eyelids closed and see the little gray-black specks moving around.

These are little strands of jelly that clump up in your eyeball and cast shadows onto your retina. They are probably the things closest to us that we can still see in the physical world. Cool, huh?

It's sometimes helpful to be proficient in this physical practice because of the parallels with being and becoming. Can you hold your perfection of being in total focus while things become infinitely different at all times?

Can you hold godly sorrow and the rest of the Lord at the same time? Can the emotional landscape become a thousand things while you rest as the open field that hasn't budged at all?

· Soften

This one is less of a game and more of a mantra. One of my teachers, Geoff, summed up the heart of this book's message when he said, "Just soften up and be here."

I usually try to soften physically, emotionally, mentally, and completely (meaning on the deepest layer of my being that I can currently sense—as awareness itself). Softening lets experience in, lets it happen. Being here keeps us in the moment, fully present.

It's a powerful combo that is deep medicine for the moments of life that keep tripping us up.

ACKNOWLEDGEMENTS

I've had an amazing team to help with this project. First and foremost, my wife, Anna, has been a constant source of fresh learning, support, and non-judgmental awareness in my life. I choose you.

Thank you to my local ward in Bella Vista, Arkansas, for being a concrete reminder of the ever-present hands of God that keep all of life in flow. The local study group that helped beta test the project are my lovely parents, Wynn and Jocelyn Peterson, as well as friends Mike and Rachelle Hiatt, Leslie and Kelly Andreasen, and Lisa and Steve Anderson. You're a generous bunch and I'm deeply touched by your engagement with the project. Thank you Haymitch, Lisa, and Jon for sharing a unique slice of your wholeness experience. Thank you Mamie Payne and Michelle Larson for never-ending trust and acceptance in all of our interactions and collaboration.

Jon Ogden, you were invaluable to the initial framing and clarifying of key concepts. Angela Harger, your editing was top notch; much of the readability and flow of the book is due to your hard work. Lori Forsyth, thank you for all the final edits and magical finishing touch. Heidi Robertson (my sister), you did incredible work on the cover design—thank you for your detailed, creative, and collaborative soul, in addition to the precision in rhetoric and word choices you offered for the main text.

All my love and thanks to Geoff, Abigail, and my GTC cohort for showing me how awakened wholeness shows up in relationships. Thank you John Kesler for trust, flexibility, and your sacred conduct. Deep bow to Thomas McConkie for keen mentorship and endless generosity of spirit. Heartfelt gratitude to Dustin DiPerna for integrity, walking ahead, and pointing out ground, path, and fruition. May there always be students; may there always be teachers.

CONTACT

For more info, coaching, resources, or simply a desire to connect around this topic, feel free to visit paulwpeterson.com/wholeness.

www.ingramcontent.com/pod-product-compliance
Lightning Source LLC
LaVergne TN
LVHW041219080426
835508LV00011B/1004